Engaging God's Word

Luke

Engage Bible Studies

Tools That Transform

Engage Bible Studies

an imprint of

 COMMUNITY BIBLE STUDY

Engaging God's Word: Luke

Copyright © 2012 by Community Bible Study. All rights reserved.

ISBN 978-1-62194-008-1

Published by Community Bible Study
790 Stout Road
Colorado Springs, CO 80921-3802
1-800-826-4181
www.communitybiblestudy.org

Contents

Introduction

Welcome to the life-changing adventure of engaging with God's Word!
Whether this is the first time you've opened a Bible or you've studied
the Scriptures all your life, good things are in store for you. Studying
the Bible is unlike any other kind of study you have ever done. That's
because the Word of God is *"living and active"* (Hebrews 4:12) and
transcends time and cultures. The earth and heavens as we know them
will one day pass away, but God's Word never will (Mark 13:31). It's
as relevant to your life today as it was to the people who wrote it down
centuries ago. And the fact that God's Word is living and active means
that reading God's Word is always meant to be a personal experience.
God's Word is not just dead words on a page—it is page after page
of living, powerful words—so get ready, because the time you spend
studying the Bible in this *Engaging God's Word* course will be life-
transforming!

Why Study the Bible?

Some Christians read the Bible because they know they're supposed to.
It's a good thing to do, and God expects it. And all that's true! However,
there are many additional reasons to study God's Word. Here are just
some of them.

We get to know God through His Word. Our God is a relational God
who knows us and wants us to know Him. The Scriptures, which He
authored, reveal much about Him: how He thinks and feels, what His
purposes are, what He thinks about us, how He views the world He
made, what He has planned for the future. The Bible shows us God's
many attributes—His kindness, goodness, justice, love, faithfulness,
mercy, compassion, creativity, redemption, sovereignty, and so on. As
we get to know Him through His Word, we come to love and trust Him.

God speaks to us through His Word. One of the primary ways God speaks to us is through His written Word. Don't be surprised if, as you read the Bible, certain parts nearly jump off the page at you, almost as if they'd been written with you in mind. God is the Author of this incredible book, so that's not just possible, it's likely! Whether it is to find comfort, warning, correction, teaching, or guidance, always approach God's Word with your spiritual ears open (Isaiah 55:3) because God, your loving heavenly Father, has things He wants to say to you.

God's Word brings life. Just about everyone wants to learn the secret to "the good life." And the good news is, that secret is found in God's Word. Don't think of the Bible as a bunch of rules. Viewing it with that mindset is a distortion. God gave us His Word because as our Creator and the Creator of the universe, He alone knows how life was meant to work. He knows that love makes us happier than hate, that generosity brings more joy than greed, and that integrity allows us to rest more peacefully at night than deception does. God's ways are not always "easiest" but they are the way to life. As the Psalmist says, *"If Your law had not been my delight, I would have perished in my affliction. I will never forget Your precepts, for by them You have given me life"* (Psalm 119:92-93).

God's Word offers stability in an unstable world. Truth is an ever-changing negotiable for many people in our culture today. But building your life on constantly changing "truth" is like building your house on shifting sand. God's Word, like God Himself, never changes. What He says was true yesterday, is true today, and will still be true a billion years from now. Jesus said, *"Everyone then who hears these words of Mine and does them will be like a wise man who built his house on the rock"* (Matthew 7:24).

God's Word helps us to pray effectively. When we read God's Word and get to know what He is really like, we understand better how to pray. God answers prayers that are according to His will. We discover His will by reading the Bible. First John 5:14-15 tells us that *"this is the confidence that we have toward Him, that if we ask anything according to His will He hears us. And if we know that He hears us in whatever we ask, we know that we have the requests that we have asked of Him."*

How to Get the Most out of *Engaging God's Word*

Each *Engaging God's Word* study contains key elements that have been carefully designed to help you get the most out of your time in God's Word. Slightly modified for your study-at-home success, this approach is very similar to the tried-and-proven Bible study method that Community Bible Study has used with thousands of men, women, and children across the United States and around the world for nearly 40 years. There are some basic things you can expect to find in each course in this series.

- ❖ Lesson 1 provides an overview of the Bible book (or books) you will study and questions to help you focus, anticipate, and pray about what you will be learning.

- ❖ Every lesson contains questions to answer on your own, commentary that reviews and clarifies the passage, and three special sections called "Apply what you have learned," "Think about" and "Personalize this lesson."

- ❖ Some lessons contain memory verse suggestions.

Whether you plan to use *Engaging God's Word* on your own or with a group, here are some suggestions that will help you enjoy and receive the most benefit from your study.

Spread out each lesson over several days. Your *Engaging God's Word* lessons were designed to take a week to complete. Spreading out your study rather than doing it all at once allows time for the things God is teaching you to sink in and for you to practice applying them.

Pray each time you read God's Word. The Bible is a book unlike any other because God Himself inspired it. The same Spirit who inspired the human authors who wrote it will help you to understand and apply it if you ask Him to. So make it a practice to ask Him to make His Word come alive to you every time you read it.

Read the whole passage covered in the lesson. Before plunging into the questions, take time to read the specific chapter or verses that will be covered in that lesson. Doing this will give you important context for the whole lesson. Reading the Bible in context is an important principle in interpreting it accurately.

Begin learning the memory verse. Learning Scripture by heart requires discipline, but the rewards far outweigh the effort. Memorizing a verse allows you to recall it whenever you need it—for personal encouragement and direction, or to share with someone else. Consider writing the verse on a sticky note or index card that you can post where you will see it often or carry with you to review during the day. Reading and re-reading the verse often—out loud when possible—is a simple way to commit it to memory.

Re-read the passage for each section of questions. Each lesson is divided into sections so that you study one small part of Scripture at a time. Before attempting to answer the questions, review the verses that the questions will cover.

Answer the questions without consulting the Commentary or other reference materials. There is great joy in having the Holy Spirit teach you God's Word on your own, without the help of outside resources. Don't cheat yourself of the delight of discovery by reading the Commentary prematurely. Wait until after you've completed the lesson.

Repeat the process for all the question sections.

Prayerfully consider the "Apply what you have learned," marked with the 📌 push pin symbol. The vision of Community Bible Study is not to just gain knowledge about the Bible, but to be transformed by it. For this reason, each set of questions closes with a section that encourages you to apply what you are learning. Usually this section involves action—something for you to do. As you practice these suggestions, your life will change.

Read the Commentary. *Engaging God's Word* commentaries are written by theologians whose goal is to help you understand the context of what you are studying as it relates to the rest of Scripture, God's character, and what the passage means for your life. Of necessity, the commentaries include the author's interpretations. While interesting and helpful, keep in mind that the Commentary is simply one person's understanding of what these passages mean. Other godly men and women have views that are also worth considering.

Pause to contemplate each "Think about" section, marked with the notepad symbol. These features, embedded in the Commentary, offer a place to pause and consider some of the principles being brought out by the text. They provide excellent ideas to journal about or to discuss with other believers, especially those doing the study with you.

Jot down insights or prayer points from the "Personalize this lesson" marked with the ☑ check box symbol. While the "Apply what you have learned" section focuses on doing, the "Personalize this lesson" section focuses on becoming. Spiritual transformation is not just about doing right things and refraining from doing wrong things—it is about changing from the inside out. To be transformed means letting God change our hearts so that our attitudes, emotions, desires, reactions, and goals are increasingly like Jesus'. Often this section will discuss something that you cannot do in your own strength—so your response will usually be something to pray about. Remember that becoming more Christ-like is not just a matter of trying harder—it requires God's empowerment.

A Gospel to the Gentile World
Luke 1:1-4

Luke wanted his readers to see Jesus as truly God and truly man. Luke quotes Jesus using the term *"Son of Man"* nearly 30 times to refer to Himself. But he also quotes demons crying out for mercy as they declare to Jesus, *"You are the Son of God!"* (4:41), and records Jesus performing many miracles that could be attributed only to God. As you embark on this study of Luke's Gospel, you will be studying the life of the Perfect Man who was perfect because He was God in a human body—*"the Son of Man [who] came to seek and save the lost"* (Luke 19:10).

In this marvelous Gospel written by a Gentile and addressed specifically to a Gentile, Luke will make the following key points to his readers:

❖ Everything about Jesus' life fulfills Old Testament Scripture.

❖ Jesus' genealogy traces back to Adam, indicating His kinship with all humans.

❖ Although Jesus would extend the offer of His kingdom beyond the people of Israel, He nonetheless showed great respect in keeping the Hebrew festivals and preaching in synagogues.

❖ Jesus performed many miracles, but the greatest was when He told the paralyzed man, *"Your sins are forgiven you"* (5:20), and the *"sinner"* woman, *"Your sins are forgiven"* (7:48).

❖ Jesus emphasizes that discipleship is difficult (9:58; 12:49-53; 14:25-32).

❖ Jesus also emphasizes the Father's great love for the lost (chapter 15).

❖ Jesus reveals both the present and future aspects of His kingdom (17:20-21; 19:11-27).

❖ Jesus is the Risen Lord (chapter 24)!

The apostle Paul would later write to the church in Rome, *"I am not
ashamed of the gospel, for it is the power of God for salvation to everyone who
believes, to the Jew first and also to the Greek"* (Romans 1:16). In Luke's
subsequent document (the book of Acts, see specifically Acts 1:8), he
records the gospel's progress as it spread from Jerusalem (Jews) to Judea
and Samaria (partial Jews), and to the end of the earth (Gentiles).

1. Why do you think God chose Luke to write this account of Jesus
    aimed primarily at Gentile readers?

    _____

    _____

    _____

2. Why do you think Jesus showed such respect for the Jewish
    people who ultimately would reject Him?

    _____

    _____

    _____

*Much of the Old Testament records God's dealings with one nation—Israel.
That doesn't mean that for all that time God was unconcerned with everyone
else. Throughout the Old Testament God was pointing to the arrival of His
Son as the Savior for all people—regardless of social status or ethnicity. As
you begin this study of Luke's Gospel, will you—and your study group, if you
are part of one—ask God to open your spiritual eyes to see His great love for
the lost near you and throughout the world?*

A Gospel to the Gentile World
Luke 1:1-4

The gospels of Matthew, Mark, and Luke are called the Synoptic Gospels because they have a similar point of view on the events of Jesus' life. John wrote his gospel later, from a different perspective. Matthew portrays Jesus as the Messiah; Mark, as the Servant of God; John, as the Son of God. But Luke introduces Jesus as the Son of Man, the divine Savior. Luke has more details about Jesus' earthly life than the other Gospels.

The Author and His Sources

It is generally accepted that Luke wrote the third Gospel as well as the book of Acts. Both books are addressed to *"most excellent Theophilus"* (Luke 1:1-4; Acts 1:1-2) and describe Jesus' life and ongoing ministry in the world. Luke's Gospel portrays Jesus as Savior; the book of Acts tells of His apostles' mission. Luke may have had access to Mark's Gospel (written earlier) and to one of Matthew's sources. Some incidents recorded here appear in Matthew, Mark, or both; others are found nowhere else, which shows that Luke had unique material gathered on his own. He also knew Peter, Andrew, John, the other disciples, and Jesus' relative James, who later served as bishop of the Jerusalem church. Luke may have heard of Jesus' encounters with Herod from Joanna, a follower of Jesus, whose husband, Chuza, managed Herod's household (Luke 8:3). Many scholars believe Jesus' mother, Mary, also gave Luke information. She could have told him about Jesus birth, and His visit to the temple.

Accounts Found Only in Luke's Gospel

The material in 1:1-3:20 is unique to Luke's Gospel, as are these miracles: the catch of fish (5:4-11); the widow's dead son raised at Nain (7:11-15); healings of the crippled woman (13:11-13), the man with dropsy (14:1-4), and the ten lepers (17:11-19). Parables found only in Luke are those about the moneylender (7:41-43); Good Samaritan (10:30-37); needy friend (11:5-8); rich fool (12:16-21); unfruitful fig tree (13:6-9); lowest seat at the feast (14:7-14); great banquet (14:16-24); cost of discipleship (14:28-33); lost coin (15:8-10); prodigal son (15:11-32); shrewd manager (16:1-8); rich man and Lazarus (16:19-31); master and his servant (17:7-10); persistent widow (18:2-8); and the Pharisee and tax collector (18:10-14).

Gospel to the Gentiles

A careful historian with an excellent command of the Greek language, Luke writes for Gentiles, emphasizing that salvation through Jesus Christ is available to all. He traces Jesus' genealogy back to Adam, the father of all people. All four Gospels include references to Isaiah 40:3, but only Luke includes Isaiah 40:5, which states: *"And the glory of the Lord shall be revealed, and all flesh shall see it."* Clearly, his purpose is to present Jesus Christ to the Gentiles as the Savior of all people—Jew or Gentile.

Unique Aspects of Luke's Gospel

Luke's record of Mary's offering at the temple (2:21-24) and the Beatitudes (6:20-26) shows his consideration for the poor. He demonstrates concern for social justice in his accounts of the rich fool (12:13-21), the command not to worry about daily needs (12:22-34), the widow's offering (21:1-4), and Judas' betrayal of Jesus for money (22:1-6). Luke portrays God's love as embracing the disreputable, the outcast, and the socially undesirable: Jesus calls a tax collector to be His disciple (5:27-32), is anointed by a sinful woman (7:36-39), and heals a boy with an evil spirit (9:37-43). The Good Samaritan helps someone in need (10:25-37). Jesus heals the blind beggar (18:35-43) and goes to the home of a despised tax collector (19:1-10). Luke records more incidents of Jesus in prayer than any other Gospel writer. He shows Jesus praying in the great moments of His life: at His baptism (3:21), before His first confrontation with the Pharisees (5:16), before choosing His disciples (6:12-13), before Peter's confession (9:18-20), at the Mount of Transfiguration (9:28-29), and on the Cross (23:46). Seeing His example, the disciples ask, *"Lord, teach us to pray."* His response is known as "The Lord's Prayer" (11:2-4). He also taught them to persevere in prayer.

Think about how Jesus serves as our example too. If God's Son found it important to pray, how much more vital is it for us to do so? Make it an objective to know God better through a life of prayer.

The Prologue of Luke's Gospel

Luke intended to present Jesus as Savior of the world, choosing and arranging his material accordingly. His introduction indicates his purpose: to write an account specifically to convince Theophilus, likely a Roman official, of the truth about Jesus. Because high-ranking Romans respected all physicians, Luke had an unusual opportunity to reach those in political power. He had access to written works about Jesus, and also interviewed *"eyewitnesses and ministers of the word"* (1:2). The term *"orderly"* (1:3) means *a logical building of evidence* that Jesus Christ is God's Son. As a scientific historian, Luke wants readers to know the validity of what they read. Being sure of the foundation of our faith is a matter of life and death. This certainty was crucial for early Christians, who faced threats of persecution, imprisonment, torture, and execution. Luke not only proclaims the gospel of Jesus Christ, he is the first person to defend the facts of Christ's redemptive ministry to all people.

Luke's Gospel can be outlined as follows:

- ❖ A. Introduction (1:1-4)
- ❖ B. Two Birth Announcements: John the Baptist and Jesus (1:5-56)
- ❖ C. John and Jesus' Birth and Boyhood (1:57-2:52)
- ❖ D. John the Baptist's Evangelistic Ministry (3:1-20)
- ❖ E. Jesus' Preparation and Inauguration (3:21-4:13)
- ❖ F. Jesus' Public Ministry in Galilee (4:14-9:50)
- ❖ G. Jesus' Expanding Ministry East of the Jordan (9:51-18:30)
- ❖ H. Jesus' Daring Ministry in Jerusalem (18:31-21:38)
- ❖ I. Passion of the Son of Man (22:1-23:56)
- ❖ J. Appearances of the Resurrected Jesus (24:1-53)

Personalize this lesson.

✓ God has always been intimately involved with His people. We are created in His image (Genesis 1:26-27) and designed for fellowship with Him. God is the one who begins and provides the way for a relationship with Him. That way is a Person—Jesus Christ (John 14:6), the one through whom all things on earth and in heaven have been made, for whom all things exist, in whom all things are significant, and to whom all things will be united (Colossians 1:16-20). It is important to know that our Christian faith is rooted and grounded in history. As Luke indicates to Theophilus, he sought and wrote the truth about Christ's conception and birth, life and ministry, death and resurrection. God's Word is accurate and trustworthy. Luke carefully chose material to best suit his purpose—to reach the Gentile world for Christ. As God's witnesses in the world, we need to be just as sensitive to the condition of those around us. By being faithful to Jesus Christ in thought, word, and actions, we show others the eternal, unchangeable truth of the gospel. Only the Holy Spirit can change people's hearts, but He wants us to demonstrate what Jesus can accomplish in a human life.

Gabriel Brings Good News
Luke 1:5-38

❖ Luke 1:5-17—John the Baptist's Birth Foretold

1. What positive facts does Luke write about Zechariah and Elizabeth?

2. What does Luke's use of the word *but* in verse 7 lead you to conclude about their childlessness? (See also Genesis 30:1-2; Deuteronomy 7:14.)

3. What do verses 8-10 indicate about the significance of corporate worship in the life of the people?

4. Does this type of worship have significance for us today? Explain your answer.

5. What does Zechariah's reaction to the angel's appearance tell you about him?

    _____

    _____

6. What does the angel's first sentence reveal about Zechariah's prayer life?

    _____

    _____

7. What does the angel's prophecy tell you about
    a. John's character?

        _____

        _____

    b. John's ministry?

        _____

        _____

❖ Luke 1:18-25—God Fulfills a Promise

8. What is Zechariah asking for in verse 18?

    _____

    _____

9. What is the answer to this request?

    _____

    _____

10. How can you apply Zechariah's encounter with the angel to your life?

    _____

    _____

    _____

    _____

11. What are some ways God has revealed Himself to you? Please share them.

_____

_____

_____

12. What does verse 25 reveal about Elizabeth's feelings regarding her childlessness?

_____

_____

13. Compared to her previous despair, what happens to Elizabeth's state of mind?

_____

_____

14. What does this account tell you about God's timing and our prayers (1:13)?

_____

_____

❖ Luke 1:26-33—Jesus' Birth Foretold

15. How does the angel Gabriel describe Mary when he greets her?

_____

_____

16. How do we find favor with God? (See Deuteronomy 30:16.)

_____

_____

17. Because Mary knew Old Testament Scriptures, including the Messianic passages, what would Gabriel's statement in verses 31-33 mean to her? (See Isaiah 7:14; 9:6-7.)

_____

_____

18. How is Mary's reaction similar to Zechariah's, and how is it
    different?

    _____

    _____

❖ Luke 1:34-38—Mary Responds to God's Call

19. If you have an "impossible" situation in your life, does verse
    37 give you a new perspective on it? (Please share, if you are
    comfortable doing so.)

    _____

    _____

20. How is Mary's declaration a worthy model for

    a. all believers?_____

    _____

    _____

    b. you?_____

    _____

    _____

Apply what you have learned. We see events
in the lives of Zechariah, Elizabeth, and Mary from
God's viewpoint as well as from a human perspective
because we have the record of what occurred. But our life
stories are still being written and we do not know everything
God does. When making requests to God, remember to
praise Him for being in control and doing what is best for
us—then trust Him.

Gabriel Brings Good News
Luke 1:5-38

Luke, a careful historian, places the start of his narrative *"in the days of Herod, king of Judea"* (1:5). Known as Herod the Great, he ruled with an iron fist, uniting his political power under the umbrella of the Roman Empire. This cruel, unpredictable pagan, appointed by the Romans in 37 BC as puppet king of the Jews, helped rebuild the temple in Jerusalem, yet later defiled it. His family history is marred by a series of murders carried out at his command. Near the end of his long reign, he ordered the murder of all boys two and under in Bethlehem (Matthew 2:16-18).

The Priesthood

Priests are descendants of Aaron from the tribe of Levi (Exodus 40:12-16) who mediate between man and God in the temple, by God's decree (Leviticus 1:4-17). Their duties include burning incense on the altar in the sanctuary or Holy Place (Exodus 30:7-8), keeping fire burning on the altar (Leviticus 6:9, 13), teaching people the Law (Leviticus 10:11), examining all who bring sacrifices to the temple, inspecting sick or unclean people, (Leviticus 13:1-17), and serving as the high court of appeals (Deuteronomy 17:8-11).

The duties of the 20,000 priests were decided by casting lots. On a certain day, the lot falls to Zechariah. While he stands praying for Israel's salvation, an angel appears, saying Elizabeth will bear him a son to be named John. John's life will signify the very turning point of history by announcing the arrival of Jesus and the coming of God's kingdom. Zechariah asks for proof that this prophecy will come true. In response, the angel gives him a sign that serves as both a proof and a scolding for his doubt—he will be unable to speak until this event occurs.

> **Think about** how easy it is to criticize Zechariah for doubting, yet our advantages are greater than his. We have the witness of Christ's life, death and resurrection, the evidence of the Holy Spirit at work, the church, and the Bible to guide, help, and correct. Do we remain firm in our faith when we don't understand our circumstances, or do we need signs? God's Word assures us of His faithfulness. Our joy is based on the fact that Jesus is with us in all we are called to endure. Trust God in the hard times, believing He will accomplish the good He has promised us.

Gabriel and Zechariah

After 400 years of apparent silence, God begins moving on behalf of His people. While Zechariah is inside the Holy Place, worshipers in the outer part of the temple also become participants in God's new beginning. The angel's words to Zechariah declare the fulfillment of prophecies for the nation of Israel: *"A voice cries: 'In the wilderness prepare the way of the Lord; make straight in the desert a highway for our God'"* (Isaiah 40:3). *"Behold, I will send you Elijah the prophet before the great and awesome day of the Lord comes"* (Malachi 4:5).

Gabriel and Mary

Six months later, God sends the angel Gabriel to Mary, a young virgin living in the Galilean village of Nazareth. Pharisees and rabbis thought of Galileans as uncultured peasants, yet Galilee was identified as the place from which God's Messiah would come (Isaiah 9:1-2, 6-7). Mary, descended from David's line and related to Elizabeth, is pledged to marry Joseph. Perhaps her family had once been important and well-known because they are connected with the priesthood; however, both she and Joseph are poor. Their year-long betrothal period, as sacred and binding as marriage, can be ended only by divorce. A physical relationship with someone else would be considered adultery.

Like Zechariah, Mary is perplexed by the angel's visit, but unlike Zechariah, who is fearful (Luke 1:12), Mary *"tried to discern what sort of greeting this might be"* (1:29). Both question the angel. Zechariah's question seems to imply, "How *can* this be done?" while Mary appears to ask, "How *will* this be done?" Mary's question is not a demand for proof, as Zechariah's is, but curiosity about how this will occur. She accepts the angel's answer graciously, knowing what the consequences of carrying the Son of God will be.

Imagine the reactions of those around her. Joseph was troubled when he heard of Mary's condition; only divine intervention stopped his plan to quietly divorce her. Her fellow villagers surely wondered about her sudden pregnancy before the actual wedding. She would have found it hard to explain what had taken place, and many would not believe her. Consider the ridicule and humiliation she must have suffered. Also, according to the Law, if an engaged virgin had a relationship with another man, she was to be stoned to death (Deuteronomy 22:23).

The angel Gabriel does not make everything perfectly clear to Mary. He tells her the Holy Spirit will come upon her and the power of the Most High will overshadow her. These are very mysterious words, yet Mary simply accepts by faith what the angel says. It was not important that she understand, nor is it necessary for us to comprehend everything God is doing. It is, however, our responsibility to trust Him to work out what we do not know and to be obedient to what He has revealed to us.

Angels in the Bible

Though the Greeks and Romans to whom Luke writes do not believe in angels, he opens his Gospel with the presence and ministry of an angel, identified as Gabriel. The Bible records many instances of angels appearing, indicating that their presence during both Old and New Testament times was common. In the first instance, an angel appears to the handmaid of a patriarch's wife (Genesis 16:7). The Hebrew word for *angel* means *messenger*. Throughout Scripture angels minister to those in leadership positions: Moses (Exodus 23:20, 23), Elijah (1 Kings 19:5-7), David (Psalm 34:7), Jesus (John 1:51), and Peter (Acts 5:19; 12:7), as well as to believers in general. *"Are they not all ministering spirits sent out to serve for the sake of those who are to inherit salvation?"* (Hebrews 1:14). Because angels are messengers and ministering spirits, they are not to be worshiped.

Personalize this lesson.

☑ Gabriel brought good news, not only to Zechariah and Mary, but to all people of every race and nation throughout history—including us. This good news is as relevant now as it was then. The good news is that God is intimately associated with His people. Although we cannot see God, He is with us. He hears and answers our prayers, calms our fears, and builds our confidence in Him. Through a miraculous process that gave Him both divine and human parentage, God became one of us. He is our great and glorious ruler, our King, who lives and reigns forever. Do we believe this good news? Do we, like Elizabeth, respond by acknowledging what God has done for us? Do we, like Mary, accept His divine plan and offer ourselves to Him in obedience? Or do we, like Zechariah, doubt that this good news could be for us? How can you respond today in obedience and praise?

Praise and Prophecy
Luke 1:39-80

Memorize God's Word: Luke 1:46-47.

❖ Luke 1:39-45—Mary Visits Elizabeth

1. What does Mary do in response to her belief in Gabriel's news about Elizabeth?

    _____

    _____

2. How does the Holy Spirit reveal Himself through Elizabeth?

    _____

    _____

3. To whom does the blessing in verse 45 apply?

    _____

❖ Luke 1:46-56—Mary's Song of Praise

4. What do the words *"my soul magnifies the Lord"* (1:46) mean to you?

    _____

    _____

5. What reasons does Mary give for rejoicing in God?

    _____

    _____

6. How might obedience to God involve both blessing and cost?

    _____

    _____

7. Beginning with verse 50, what change takes place in Mary's song?

    _____

    _____

8. How would you describe God's activities as seen in verses 51-53?

    _____

    _____

9. What are the implications of these verses in today's world?

    _____

    _____

❖ Luke 1:57-66—John the Baptist's Birth

10. How are Zechariah and Elizabeth faithful to the Jewish Law?
    (See Genesis 17:9-19.)

    _____

    _____

11. How do their neighbors and relatives react to their choice of a
    name for the baby?

    _____

    _____

12. What is Zechariah's response (1:63)?

    _____

    _____

13. How does Zechariah's response in verse 64 compare to his
    earlier attitude? (See 1:18-20.)

    _____

    _____

14. How do the neighbors and relatives

    a. fulfill God's prophecy about the baby's birth (1:14, 58)?

    _____

    _____

    b. show reverence in response to Zechariah's miraculous recovery?

    _____

    _____

    c. reveal a continuing curiosity about John?

    _____

    _____

❖ Luke 1:67-75—Zechariah's Song

15. How are Zechariah's prophecy and God's covenant with Abraham (Genesis 22:16-18) related?

    _____

    _____

    _____

16. What does Zechariah indicate would result from God's people being saved from their enemies (1:71-75)?

    _____

    _____

    _____

❖ Luke 1:76-80—The Song Continues

17. How will the child's predicted title in verse 76 relate to his special calling?

    _____

    _____

    _____

18. *Mercy* is defined as *kind, compassionate treatment of a person or people.* How is God's mercy associated with salvation, the forgiveness of sins, light, and peace?

_____

_____

19. a.   To whom does Zechariah refer when he speaks of *"those who sit in darkness"* (1:79)? (See also Isaiah 9:1-2; John 3:16-21.)

_____

_____

    b.   How does this verse apply to us today?

_____

_____

20. What balance does Luke note in the child's development, and why is it important?

_____

_____

_____

Apply what you have learned. Although she knew the challenges that lay ahead, Mary responded to God's work in her life with excitement and thanksgiving. Looking at God's faithfulness in the past, she had faith that He would take care of her future. When God asks us to step out of our comfort zone, it's easy to get caught up in our feelings and fears. But Mary's prayer reminds us to look instead to God's faithfulness and trust Him to take care of us. Are there any areas of your life where God might want to work in new ways? Talk to Him about it. Take comfort knowing He is more than strong enough to take you where He wants you to go, and His plans for you are perfect.

Praise and Prophecy
Luke 1:39-80

The beginning of Luke chapter 1 records the angel Gabriel's visits—first to Zechariah to announce the coming birth of a son to be named John, and later to Mary to tell her she will give birth to God's Son. The remainder of the chapter includes the account of John the Baptist's birth, and Mary and Zechariah's songs of praise to God.

Mary Visits Elizabeth

Soon after Gabriel's visit, Mary travels to the hill country of Judea to visit her relative Elizabeth, who had been infertile, but *"in her old age"* (Luke 1:36) is pregnant. The angel tells Mary, *"Nothing will be impossible with God"* (1:37). On hearing Mary's greeting, Elizabeth is filled with the Holy Spirit, and the baby leaps inside her. Jewish tradition called for young people to respect the elderly, but here the older woman defers to the younger. Elizabeth recognizes that Mary is carrying in her womb the Messiah, the Savior of the world. They have much to share; their meeting is joyful and significant. Elizabeth's blessing and Mary's hymn of praise beautifully express their recognition that, through their children, God will fulfill ancient promises to Israel and bring salvation to all people.

Mary's Song of Praise

Mary's song reveals her knowledge of God's Word. She calls God her *"Savior"* (1:47) and acknowledges His favor in choosing her to be the Messiah's mother. She praises God, knowing that only He could enable such unlikely women—one too old, the other a virgin—each to have a child. She recounts the times God helped Israel and recognizes that the soon-coming Savior, her Son, is the One promised to Abraham (Genesis 22:17-18). She attests to God's sovereignty in the affairs of people and nations. The fulfillment of this promise is evidence of God's mercy.

Mary's prophetic song declares that God cares not only about Israel, but about the entire world (John 3:16). Mary stays with Elizabeth about three months. By the time she returns home, obviously pregnant, she knows she will have to face Joseph, her family, friends, and neighbors— and speculation and gossip.

Think about how God's timing is different from ours. Elizabeth was an older woman who longed for a baby. Mary was a young virgin about to marry. From a human perspective, both were pregnant at "inconvenient" times in their lives. When we least expect it, God invades our lives, asking our obedience in seemingly impossible situations. Mary may have been afraid as she returned to Nazareth, but perhaps she recalled God's word to Joshua: *"Be strong and courageous. Do not be frightened ... for the Lord your God is with you wherever you go"* (Joshua 1:9).

John the Baptist's Birth

As Gabriel had prophesied, Elizabeth gives birth to a son, and everyone rejoices. The time of circumcision, which coincides with the child's official naming, is one of celebration. Usually, the first son is named after his father. But Elizabeth insists on calling him *John*, which means *God is gracious or God's gift*. Thinking the name is Elizabeth's idea, her relatives and friends ask Zechariah what he wants to name the baby. Still unable to speak, he writes: *"His name is John"* (Luke 1:63). Instantly, he regains his ability to speak. By this time, all their family, friends, and neighbors are convinced that God has indeed been personally involved in this child's birth.

Zechariah's Song of Prophecy

Zechariah, filled with the Holy Spirit, proclaims God's liberating intervention. How joyful he must have been, knowing God had chosen his son to prepare the way for the Messiah (Isaiah 40:1-3; Malachi 3:1). Zechariah's words, like Mary's, reveal knowledge of Old Testament prophesies concerning Israel. He proclaims the coming of a mighty Savior as *"a horn of salvation"* (Luke 1:69), symbolizing power and victory. The Messiah would be a powerful deliverer from David's line (Psalm 132:17-18). Would he be a political Messiah or the Christ of our salvation? Based on verses 77-78, Zechariah's prophecy points to the Savior of all people, the King of kings who would govern the entire human race (Revelation 19:11-16). Zechariah's prophetic statement is based on Old Testament prophets' predictions, recalling God's promise to Abraham and his offspring *"to show the mercy promised to our fathers and to remember His holy covenant"* (Luke 1:72).

Living in an occupied country, Zechariah and his fellow Jews might have interpreted verse 74 to mean liberation from Roman rule, but it could also mean deliverance from spiritual enemies. Zechariah then speaks of John, who would preach a baptism of repentance for the forgiveness of sins, pointing his disciples to the One who could give them eternal life. Usually, a prophet's task was to give God's counsel or message to others. God occasionally inspired prophets to predict phenomenal events. Note Malachi's prophecy of the coming of Messiah's forerunner (Malachi 4:5-6). Zechariah surely knew that passage, and with Gabriel's words fresh in his mind, he likely understands his son's mission (John 1:23, 29).

God promises to guide us and grant us a peace beyond our understanding, *"to give light to those who sit in darkness and in the shadow of death, to guide our feet into the way of peace"* (Luke 1:79). God offers a salvation that meets every person's needs. This is the good news John the Baptist proclaimed and Jesus embodied and made available to all. Zechariah's hymn of praise and prophecy results from an overflowing experience with God. John the Baptist, his son, is to be the Messiah's forerunner, and in Zechariah's lifetime the Messiah will come!

John the Baptist Grows Up

Luke ends this chapter by saying John grew physically and spiritually. While John likely moved to the wilderness as an adult, Jesus lived in Nazareth and worked as an apprentice carpenter. John the Baptist and Jesus grew up in the same manner as other young men living in Judea. As we read in Luke's Gospel, we will see the working out of God's salvation. By the end of this study, may we say with the apostle John: *"We have seen His glory, glory as of the only Son from the Father, full of grace and truth"* (John 1:14).

Personalize this lesson.

☑ Mary, Elizabeth, and Zechariah all praised God, but Zechariah's praise is especially interesting. What a contrast to his doubt when the angel told him he and his wife would have a son. In his story, we see the transition from words of unbelief to prayers of assurance, faith, and praise. The songs of praise reveal how God's words, such a part of these servants' lives, naturally flowed out of their hearts in praise to Him. As we study God's Word, it takes root in our lives and becomes part of us (2 Timothy 2:15). Ask God to etch His Word on your heart so that praise naturally pours from your mouth as you see Him fulfilling His promises in your life.

Jesus' Birth and Boyhood
Luke 2

Memorize God's Word: Luke 2:11.

❖ Matthew 1:18-25—An Angel Appears to Joseph

1. What does this passage reveal about Joseph's personal character, his respect for Mary, and his allegiance to God?

   _____

   _____

2. How would Joseph's character be important in Jesus' life?

   _____

   _____

3. What are the two names given to Mary's child (1:21-23), what does each mean, and how do these names offer us hope?

   _____

   _____

   _____

❖ Luke 2:1-7—Jesus' Birth

4. Read Matthew 2:1-6. What is the significance of Bethlehem to Joseph, God, and Herod?

   _____

   _____

   _____

5. Why do you think Luke dates the first census so precisely
    (Luke 2:1-2)?

    _____

    _____

6. What does 2:1-4 tell you about how God works, and how does
    this knowledge encourage you personally?

    _____

    _____

    _____

❖ Luke 2:8-20—A Special Birth Announcement

7. How would you describe the work, social standing, and/or
    spiritual condition of the people to whom the angel announces
    Jesus' birth?

    _____

    _____

    _____

8. Why do you think the angel appears specifically to these people?

    _____

    _____

9. Why is the angel's news both "good" and a "great joy" (2:10) to
    all people?

    _____

    _____

10. Why is the announcement of Jesus' birth followed by a song
    (2:14) expressing

    a. *"glory to God"?* _____

        _____

    b. peace to those *"with whom He is pleased"?* _____

        _____

11. What do the shepherds do in response to the angel's news?

_____

_____

12. What do these actions show about their attitude toward the angel's message?

_____

_____

_____

13. Why does Mary react the way she does to these events?

_____

_____

_____

❖ Luke 2:21-38—Jesus Welcomed in the Temple

14. Read Leviticus 12:3, 6-8. How do Mary and Joseph

   a.   obey Jewish Law? _____

   _____

   _____

   b.   reveal their financial state? (See Luke 2:24; Leviticus 12:8.)

   _____

   _____

15. Who is Simeon, and who prompts him to go to the temple courts?

_____

_____

16. In what way is Simeon's prophecy similar to Zechariah's? (See Luke 1:77-79; 2:30-32.)

_____

_____

_____

17. How does Anna's response to Jesus reflect her relationship with God?

_____

_____

❖ Luke 2:39-52—The Boy Jesus at the Temple

18. How do Mary and Joseph show their devotion and/or responsibility to God and to Jesus?

_____

_____

19. Compare Jesus' words in verse 49 with Mary's question in verse 48. What clue does this give to Jesus' understanding of His relationship to God and His mission in the world?

_____

_____

20. What do verses 50-51 tell you about Jesus?

_____

_____

Apply what you have learned. The Christmas story contradicts all our ideas about what is suitable for a person of high position. The ruler over the house of Jacob was born in a stable. All the people involved in Jesus' birth would be seen as "nobodies" in the eyes of Israel's spiritual rulers as well as the Roman government. It doesn't matter to God what power you have in your job or community. God looks at the place you have made for Him in your life. Will you take some time now to consider the place you have made for Him in your life?

Jesus' Birth and Boyhood
Luke 2

Jesus' Birth

Jesus' birth is recorded in the Gospels of Matthew and Luke. Writing mainly for Jewish readers, Matthew includes Jesus' genealogy through Joseph's lineage. Hearing Mary is with child, Joseph is grieved by what appears to be Mary's unfaithfulness. Nevertheless, unwilling to *"put her to shame"* (Matthew 1:19), he plans to divorce her quietly. Before he acts on his plan, *"an angel of the Lord appear*[s] *to him in a dream"* (1:20), telling him to wed Mary. He obeys, knowing the baby will arrive too soon after their marriage to avoid gossip.

Luke records the Savior's birth in great detail. Caesar Augustus is emperor of the Roman Empire, which encompasses the civilized world. Caesar thinks he is in control when he orders a census. He does not realize that, through him, God is fulfilling a prophecy written 650 years earlier: *"But you, O Bethlehem … from you shall come forth for Me One who is to be ruler in Israel, whose coming forth is from of old, from ancient days"* (Micah 5:2). God's timing is perfect—the world into which the Messiah is born has good roads, fast ships, and efficient communication. The good news of the Savior can travel fast.

For tax purposes, a census required each citizen to register in his ancestral town. Joseph and Mary, both of King David's lineage, travel 70 miles to Bethlehem. On arrival, *"there was no place for them in the inn"* (Luke 2:7). The lack of room is further evidence that God is in control. They find shelter in humble surroundings, and there Mary gives birth and lays Jesus in a manger. As Mary tenderly cares for the infant Jesus, angels announce His birth—the greatest news in all history—to shepherds in a nearby field.

The shepherds respond to the angel's message by setting out to find Jesus. They share what they have been told about the child, amazing all who hear their account (Luke 2:17-18). Mary treasures these events and ponders them in her heart. The shepherds return to their fields *"glorifying and praising God"* (2:20).

Long-Expected Jesus

As observant Jews, Mary and Joseph have Jesus circumcised on His eighth day and wait 40 days (Leviticus 12:2-8) before going to the temple in Jerusalem to offer a sacrifice and dedicate Jesus to God. As the family arrives, Simeon and Anna are in the temple courts. Simeon, the first to publicly express faith in Jesus as Savior, Christ, and Lord, says many will oppose Christ (Isaiah 8:14). Mary will also experience sorrow, as if a sword has pierced her soul. When Anna, who prays and fasts constantly in the temple, sees Jesus, she thanks God and speaks of Jesus to all who are looking for the Messiah.

The Holy Spirit reveals to Simeon and Anna Jesus' identity as Messiah. We can acknowledge Him as Savior and Lord of our lives only by the Holy Spirit's leading (2 Corinthians 4:4, 6). When God opens our minds, it is our responsibility to respond.

Think about how God chose lowly shepherds to hear the news of Jesus' arrival on earth. In the Judaic culture, shepherds were perpetually unclean. Daily, they came into contact with ceremonial impurity. Their sheep grazed across the property of others and they could never make reimbursement to all the proper owners as rabbinic law would dictate. Distrusted and feared, they were social outcasts, not even allowed to bear witness in court. Yet God made sure they were the first to know of the Savior's birth! From the very beginning, God included the despised and rejected in His redemptive plan. And He still delights in using unlikely people to tell His story (1 Corinthians 1:26-29).

The Childhood of Jesus

Joseph and Mary probably do not return to Nazareth immediately after the wise men appear. The couple is in Bethlehem in Judea when an angel tells Joseph to flee with his family to Egypt to escape the massacre of all male infants in Bethlehem, ordered by Herod the Great (Matthew 2:13-14). After Herod dies, the angel tells Joseph to return to Israel. The family settles in Nazareth in Galilee, fulfilling prophecy that Christ would be a Nazarene (Matthew 2:19-23).

Luke, the only Gospel writer to mention Jesus' boyhood, says that He grew mentally, physically, emotionally, and spiritually. Jesus is thoroughly human and thoroughly God. While retaining His deity, He walked in His humanity on earth (Philippians 2:7), undergoing the normal human growth and development process: *"Jesus increased in wisdom and in stature and in favor with God and man"* (Luke 2:52). The Greek word for *favor* means *acceptable, agreeable,* and *graceful.* Surely Jesus would have demonstrated these character traits during His years of growing to manhood. As an adult, the Lord Jesus showed people how to live in harmony with and dependence on God. His right relationship with God kept Him in a right relationship with others.

Luke notes an incident in the temple when Jesus is 12 years old. At that age, a Jewish boy is considered a man—a *son of the Law* (*Bar Mitzvah*), responsible for religious duties. How could Joseph and Mary fail to realize that Jesus is not with them on the journey home? In that era, men and women, even husbands and wives, were forbidden to be physically close to each other in public. Mary must have walked with other women in the caravan as Joseph moved along with the men, each thinking Jesus was with the other. Imagine their concern when they came together that night and realized Jesus was not with either of them! They most likely had to wait until the next morning to start the day-long trip back to Jerusalem. If they arrived in the evening, they may have needed to wait until the next morning to look for Jesus, which explains why it took three days to find Him. He had stayed, asking the teachers penetrating questions and responding to their questions with amazing insight.

Reacting as most mothers would, Mary scolds Jesus. He asks why they looked for Him, because He *"must be in* [His] *Father's house"* (2:49). We do not know how or when Jesus becomes aware of Himself as God's unique Son, but here He is aware of a special relationship to His heavenly Father and gently reminds Mary and Joseph of this. Even though they do not understand, Jesus obeys them and returns to Nazareth.

Personalize this lesson.

☑ Jesus Christ, the Son of the Most High, was born in the most humble of places. The ruler over Israel was laid in a manger (1:32-33; 2:7). The everlasting King was obedient to His parents (1:33; 2:51). The Son of God became the Son of Man (1:35). The One who is *"God with us"* (Matthew 1:23) understands our human condition. He created us, and He also knows the human experience of growing up and living on this earth. The Lord Jesus, who grew physically, enables us to accept and appreciate our humanity. He who increased in wisdom increases our understanding and knowledge. He who matured in favor with God brings us into a right relationship with His Father. He who developed in favor with all people helps us in our associations with others. *"For we do not have a high priest who is unable to sympathize with our weaknesses, but one who in every respect has been tempted as we are, yet without sin"* (Hebrews 4:15). For to us is born *"a Savior, who is Christ the Lord"* (Luke 2:11). *"Thanks be to God for His inexpressible gift!"* (2 Corinthians 9:15). Will you take a moment to record what this inexpressible gift means to you?

John the Baptist and Jesus
Luke 3

Memorize God's Word: Luke 2:52.

❖ Luke 3:1-6—John the Baptist Begins His Ministry

1. Why do you think Luke documents Israel's political and religious setting at the start of John the Baptist's ministry?

_____

_____

2. Concerning John the Baptist:
   a. Why do you think he lives in the wilderness?

   _____

   _____

   b. From verse 2, how is he called into ministry?

   _____

3. What is the relationship between repentance and forgiveness?

_____

_____

4. Isaiah's prophecy found in Luke 3:4-6 is highly poetic. Tell what you think he is saying by writing these verses in your own words. What significance does this message have for us today?

_____

_____

❖ Luke 3:7-14—John Preaches Repentance

5. How does John's message (Luke 3:7-9) fulfill Gabriel's prophecy about him in Luke 1:16-17?

_____

_____

6. Why is such harshness necessary?

_____

_____

7. What is good *"fruit"* (3:8)? (See also Galatians 5:22-23; Colossians 1:10.)

_____

_____

8. What is one reason some lives do not produce good fruit?

_____

_____

9. How does John's preaching (Luke 3:8-9) deal with one's responsibility to bear good fruit?

_____

_____

10. List the three groups of people who ask John for guidance, and his directions to each.

_____

_____

_____

_____

11. What does this account teach us about repentance?

_____

_____

❖ Luke 3:15-20—John Exhorts the People

12. Considering previous information in Luke 3, why do the people wonder if John is the Christ?

_____

_____

13. How does John view himself and the baptisms he has performed in relationship to the Christ?

_____

_____

14. What are the possible results of preaching in the same way John did (3:19-20; 6:22-23)?

_____

_____

15. Read Mark 6:17-20. How would you describe Herod's feelings about John?

_____

_____

16. Why does Herod put John in prison (Luke 3:19-20)?

_____

_____

❖ Luke 3:21-22—John Baptizes Jesus

17. Read Matthew 3:13-17.

   a. Why does Jesus come to be baptized even though He has never sinned?

   _____

   _____

   b. Why does John hesitate to baptize Jesus?

   _____

❖ Luke 3:23-38; read also Matthew 1:1-17—Jesus' Genealogy

18. Why is Jesus' genealogy important? (See Isaiah 9:7; Luke 1:32-33.)

_____

_____

19. What do both the Old and New Testaments record of Adam's parentage? (See Genesis 5:1-2.)

_____

_____

20. How do all people share in the way Adam was created?

_____

_____

Apply what you have learned. God is *"well pleased"* with His Son, Jesus (Luke 3:22). Because Jesus is pleasing to God, He is the One who is able to bring us to God. Indeed, we become God's own children by believing and trusting in His Son for salvation. List some people you would like to see as God's children—and then pray for them.

John the Baptist and Jesus
Luke 3

John the Baptist Begins His Ministry

Luke begins his record of Jesus' ministry with John the Baptist's emergence: *"The word of God came to John the son of Zechariah in the wilderness. And he went into all the region around the Jordan, proclaiming a baptism of repentance for the forgiveness of sins"* (3:2-3). The expression *"the word of the LORD came"* often appears in the Old Testament referring to God's prophets (Isaiah 38:4; Jeremiah 1:4; Ezekiel 3:16). John the Baptist begins his ministry 400 years after a prophetic voice was last heard in Israel. Preaching repentance and the good news that Jesus, God's sacrificial Lamb, will take away people's sin (John 1:29), John could be considered the last of the Old Testament prophets to herald God's coming kingdom.

Living in the desert, far from worldly distractions, John prays and meditates, preparing for his ministry. All obstacles to God's message must be removed from people's hearts so they can receive the truth. In Luke's day, preparations for a high official's visit included improving the road—filling in rough spots and straightening curves. In a spiritual sense, that is John's mission: to prepare hearts to receive the Messiah.

John preaches a baptism of repentance for the forgiveness of sins, a new concept for Israel. Pharisees and Sadducees strictly follow religious laws and self-righteously think they have special standing with God because they are Abraham's descendants (Luke 3:8; John 8:31-33). They baptize Gentiles who want to become Jews, but are shocked at the idea that they themselves need forgiveness for sins. They do not understand that God looks at the heart, not their ancestry, social standing, or how well they keep the Law (Romans 2:28-29). John tells the crowd to produce *"fruits in keeping with repentance"* (Luke 3:8)—words and actions must show evidence of a repentant heart and willingness to obey God. John warns them that failure to produce good fruit will result in their destruction. When the crowd asks what they should do, he gives specific answers. They must share their worldly goods. Tax collectors must not cheat. And soldiers must stop robbing others and making false accusations, and be content with their wages.

John's message brings the good news that God can redeem sinners and will forgive all who repent. Asked if he is the Christ, John denies it and speaks of one mightier than he who will baptize people with the Holy Spirit and fire. The good news will be preached fully when Jesus begins His ministry. But before they can hear His gospel message, John's task is to show people their sin and need for repentance and forgiveness. His harsh condemnation of sin is necessary, just as painful surgery is needed for healing to begin.

John proclaims a deeply convicting message in the midst of great opposition. He refuses to compromise God's moral standards and confronts Herod for his evil ways, including marrying his brother's wife. In response, Herod imprisons John. Apparently Herod never repents, so he cannot enjoy forgiveness. John is faithful to God and the eternal value of His truth. Although his life is cut short, John the Baptist finishes the work God gave him to do—he prepares the way for Jesus.

Jesus Begins His Ministry

At first John refuses to baptize Jesus (Matthew 3:13-15), knowing He is sinless and has no need for repentance (Hebrews 4:15). Through baptism, however, Jesus identifies Himself with the sinners He has come to save (John 1:29). After His baptism, Jesus begins to pray. Heaven opens, the Holy Spirit descends like a dove, and a voice from heaven says, *"You are My beloved Son; with You I am well pleased"* (Luke 3:22). In an example of the Trinity's harmony, God the Father pronounces His affirmation as the Holy Spirit, in the form of a dove, commissions Jesus, the Son.

Think about the encouragement we get from being God's children. Just as God affirmed Jesus as His Son, He acknowledges us as His children in Christ. As God spoke to Jesus, He speaks to us as we abide in Christ,

read His Word, and listen to Him through prayer. As the
Father indicated His pleasure in Jesus, He takes pleasure in
us as His children in Christ. He is our personal Lord who
ministers to each of us individually. Wherever we are, He is
with us. He will never leave us or forsake us; nothing will
ever separate us from His love (Deuteronomy 31:8;
Romans 8:38-39).

Jesus' Lineage

The only Gospel writer to indicate Jesus' and John the Baptist's ages,
Luke says *"Jesus, when He began His ministry, was about thirty years of age"*
(3:23); John is six months older. Jesus is about 33 at His crucifixion—a
conclusion drawn from the fact that He attends the annual Passover
Feast three consecutive times. John's Gospel refers to all three: the first
in 2:23; the second in 6:4; and the third in 11:55; 12:1; 13:1; 18:28, 39;
and 19:14.

Luke, a Greek himself, knows how Greeks delight in perfection, beauty,
and detail. He aims to prove Jesus is the perfect Son of Man as well as
God in the flesh. Matthew traces Jesus' line back to Abraham through
Joseph to show His Jewish lineage. But Luke traces Jesus back to Adam,
linking Him with God's original creation. Luke declares that Jesus came
for all people from all places and all historical periods.

In ancient culture, a person's lineage was traced through the father.
Luke 3:23 includes an added statement about Joseph, Jesus' legal
father. Joseph is Jacob's son by birth (Matthew 1:16) and Heli's son by
marriage. Therefore, some scholars conclude that Luke obtained his
genealogy of Jesus directly from Mary, one of his sources. Matthew's
genealogy of Jesus emphasizes His royal descent, whereas Luke
underlines His priestly lineage. Both Gospel writers show that Jesus is
descended from David, according to prophecy. Matthew's genealogy lists
David's son Solomon in Joseph's lineage; Luke lists David's son Nathan,
an ancestor of Mary. Although biblical genealogies are not meant to be
comprehensive records, they are sufficient to establish Jesus' connection
to David's bloodline as fulfillment of the Messianic prophecies.

Personalize this lesson.

☑ John brought a message of repentance from sin. Does that mean that we must be free of all sin in order to be saved? Of course not! As the apostle John told his readers, *"If we confess our sins, He is faithful and just to forgive us our sins and to cleanse us from all unrighteousness. If we say we have not sinned, we make Him a liar, and His word is not in us"* (1 John 1:9-10). Repentance from sin does not mean being utterly sinless in all our thoughts and actions—only Jesus achieved that. Repentance from sin starts with admitting sin's presence in our lives, since the first step in overcoming any predicament is admitting its existence. John wanted those who came to him for baptism to do so in sincerity, recognizing their need to change, not merely pretending like a *"brood of vipers."* That's why, when the people asked him, *"What then shall we do,"* he told them to behave in a manner that showed love for their neighbors. He wasn't telling them that helping their neighbors would save them, but it would show that they had the right attitude. Those who were not willing to actively love their neighbors were also those who would not be ready to accept the Savior. Is there a friend or neighbor you can love and help in Jesus' name this week?

Lesson 6

Temptations and Victories
Luke 4

❖ Luke 4:1-2—Jesus Is Led Into the Wilderness

1. What is the difference between being *tempted* and being *tested*? (See James 1:2-3, 13-14.)

    _____

    _____

2. Why is Jesus *"led by the Spirit in the wilderness"* (Luke 4:1) to be tempted? (See also Hebrews 4:14-16.)

    _____

    _____

3. How does Jesus' fight with temptation encourage you?

    _____

    _____

4. Read John 14:15-17, 26 and John 16:7.

    a. Who sends the Holy Spirit, and where does He reside?

    _____

    _____

    b. Record two titles for the Holy Spirit given in these verses. Explain how He ministers to a believer and helps during times of temptation.

    _____

    _____

❖ Luke 4:3-13—Jesus' Temptation

5. Compare the first temptation (4:3) with Jesus' action seen in Luke 9:13-17. What is the root of the temptation?

    _____

    _____

    _____

    _____

    _____

6. From Psalm 2:7-8, who besides Satan promises Jesus the world, and how is Jesus to attain it?

    _____

    _____

7. What is the root of the second temptation?

    _____

    _____

8. What does this passage reveal about the devil's worldly authority and his sly use of Scripture? (See also John 14:30.)

    _____

    _____

    _____

9. How does Luke 4:13 indicate Jesus' need to stay alert to the devil's schemes?

    _____

    _____

10. According to Psalm 119:11 and James 4:7, how can we resist temptation?

    _____

    _____

    _____

❖ Luke 4:14-21—Jesus Returns to Galilee and Nazareth

11. Jesus enters Galilee in the strength of the Holy Spirit. How do the people respond to Him?

_____

_____

12. Concerning Jesus' reading of the prophet Isaiah (Isaiah 61:1-2):

   a. Why would *"good news"* (the gospel) be especially preached to the poor and who would have been the captives in bondage (Luke 4:18)?

   _____

   _____

   b. In what ways does Jesus' ministry fulfill this Scripture? (See also Matthew 8:14-17; Luke 7:11-15;19:1-10.)

   _____

   _____

13. How does Jesus reveal that He is the one spoken about in Isaiah's prophecy?

_____

_____

❖ Luke 4:22-30—Jesus Is Rejected in Nazareth

14. a. After the people's initial acceptance, Jesus reveals their true thoughts. From verses 23-27, what do the people expect Jesus to do for them?

   _____

   _____

   b. Which verse indicates that they do not believe in Him or follow Him?

   _____

❖ Luke 4:31-44—Jesus Heals and Rescues

15. Demons are evil spirits who can cause people to be loud, disruptive, and physically violent. They may display knowledge of Jesus as the Son of God. Why does Jesus silence them?

_____

_____

16. Concerning Jesus' healing ministry, what kinds of healings take place?

_____

_____

_____

17. What does Jesus see as His mission?

_____

_____

Apply what you have learned. Jesus' temptation in the desert and His victory over the devil prepared Him for coming challenges. His townspeople rejected Him as Messiah and tried to kill Him. His mere presence provoked a demon's anger. He faithfully ministered through the night to those who needed healing in Capernaum. In all these situations, Jesus was victorious through the Spirit's power. When you are in difficult circumstances, remember that you, too, overcome them not by your own strength or wisdom, but by the Holy Spirit's power (Zechariah 4:6). What difficult circumstances do you face now? How can you pray about this in light of this lesson?

Lesson 6 Commentary

Temptations and Victories
Luke 4

After Jesus' public baptism, inauguration into ministry, and affirmation from God, the Spirit leads Him into the solitude of the desert. While there, He will be tempted and tested, and His devotion and obedience to God will be challenged to a degree that probably none of us will ever fully understand.

Jesus Is Led Into the Desert

Jesus fasts and prays for 40 days in the desert. In Scripture, the number 40 usually signifies a period of testing. God sent rain on the earth for 40 days and nights, testing Noah's faith, which proved true (Genesis 7:4-5). The Israelites' faith was twice tested for 40 days (Exodus 24:18; 32:7; Psalm 95:8-10) and failed. Israel's army cowered before Goliath's 40-day challenge (1 Samuel 17:16). After His resurrection, Jesus appeared to His followers for 40 days to strengthen them.

Most significant in Jesus' desert experience is His triumph over temptation by the power of the Holy Spirit, who equips Him to face Satan's attacks. God never tempts anyone with evil (James 1:13), nor will the Holy Spirit lead anyone away from the Father.

Satan Confronts Jesus

Satan uses temptations common to all humans against Jesus: *"the desires of the flesh and the desires of the eyes and pride of life"* (1 John 2:16). After a 40-day fast, Jesus is hungry. Knowing Jesus can use His power to produce food, Satan suggests that He turn a stone into bread—in effect, to abuse His God-given power for His own benefit. Jesus knows that making stones into bread would be a departure from God's way. Jesus' miracles were always for the benefit of others, never for Himself. So, quoting Deuteronomy 8:3, He resists Satan.

Next, the devil tempts Jesus with the world's temporary glory: If He will worship Satan, the ruler of the world (John 14:30), He can have all the authority and splendor of its kingdoms. Jesus replies by quoting Deuteronomy 6:13: *"Worship the Lord your God, and Him only shall you serve"* (Luke 4:8).

Think about how Jesus, at His weakest physically, withstands everything the devil throws at Him. He knows the importance of God's Word as His defense against Satan. By speaking it, He resists the evil one on spiritual grounds. In Ephesians 6:10-18, the Word of God is called *"the sword of the Spirit."* Following Jesus' example, we, too, can withstand Satan's schemes by depending on God and the Word (2 Corinthians 10:4). Make God's Word part of your life, so that when the tempter comes, you will be prepared.

The third temptation is lethal: If Jesus is truly God's Son, He can jump off the highest part of Jerusalem's temple and survive. Satan challenges Jesus' identity, and then misuses Scripture (Psalm 91:11-12). In reply, Jesus again quotes Scripture. In this way, He overcomes the devil's temptations. But this will not be the last time that Satan will attack Him.

Victories in Galilee

After His testing in the desert, Jesus begins His Galilean ministry. He draws crowds eager for His teaching and healings. Galilee was a 50- by 25-mile area along the Sea of Galilee. Its people were fishermen and farmers. Their religious life centered around the synagogue in Nazareth. Each service included prayers, a reading from the scrolls, and teaching.

Because there is no "professional" preacher, the synagogue attendant could ask anyone to teach. One day he hands the scroll to Jesus, who reads, *"The Spirit of the Lord God is upon Me, because the Lord has anointed Me to bring good news to the poor; He has sent Me to bind up the brokenhearted, to proclaim liberty to the captives, and the opening of the prison to those who are bound; to proclaim the year of the Lord's favor"* (Isaiah 61:1-2), prophetic verses perfectly describing His work.

It is a dramatic moment when Jesus closes the scroll and begins to teach.

He is indeed the bearer of good news: *"Today this scripture has been fulfilled in your hearing"* (Luke 4:21). The people are in awe, but puzzled because they know Him only as Joseph's son. Then Jesus says, *"No prophet is acceptable in his hometown"* (4:24). Aware of His healings in other places, the people expect Him to do the same in Nazareth. Instead, He cites examples of God's blessings to Gentiles when the prophets were rejected in their own country. This angers His Jewish audience, who believe they alone are God's favored people. Jesus indicates that Gentiles will share the Jews' blessings, so they try to *"throw Him down the cliff"* (4:29). But the time for His death has not yet come, so He walks away.

From Nazareth Jesus goes to Capernaum, in Galilee. In the synagogue, Jesus casts an evil spirit out of a man. The spirit asks, *"What have you to do with us, Jesus of Nazareth? Have You come to destroy us? I know who You are—the Holy One of God"* (4:34). Jesus commands him to leave the man instantly, and the evil spirit obeys. Amazed onlookers marvel at His authority and power over evil spirits. Naturally, *"reports about Him went out into every place in the surrounding region"* (4:37). The Lord then goes to Peter's home, where Peter's mother-in-law is sick. Jesus rebukes her fever, and she instantly gets up and serves Jesus and His followers—convincing evidence of His healing power.

Before the busy day is over, many people bring sick friends and family members to Jesus. Jesus' miracles—healing the sick and setting captives free—cause many to realize He is the Son of God.

The next morning Jesus goes out to the desert to pray. He never permits the day's challenges to keep Him from time with His Father. When the crowd finds Him, they beg Him to stay—what a contrast to those in Nazareth. Jesus explains that He cannot. For the first time he speaks of the *"kingdom of God"* (4:43). He is not talking about a political kingdom. The good news is that the kingdom of God can dwell in all who believe in Him and accept His words.

Personalize this lesson.

☑ James wrote, *"Let no one say when he is tempted, 'I am being tempted by God,' for God cannot be tempted with evil, and He himself tempts no one"* (James 1:13). God never tempts us, but sometimes He puts us in places in which we face temptations—as He did with Jesus. Our passage says, *"Jesus … was led by the Spirit in the wilderness for forty days, being tempted by the devil"* (Luke 4:1-2). Jesus' resolve to obey the Father's will was never in question. He faced the devil's temptations in order to show us how to face temptations. Three temptations, one answer: *"It is written."* Reading and remembering God's Word is a key element in overcoming temptations, but we can't do it all on our own. When we fail the test of a temptation, we naturally want to hide from God, but that's precisely the time to seek Him out for the forgiveness and comfort He offers (see 1 John 1:9). When you face a temptation, will you lean on His Word—*"It is written"*? If your reaction to a test is not what you think God would want, will you run *to Him* rather than *away from Him*? He wants you to succeed. Take time this week to contemplate Jude 24-25: *"Now to Him who is able to keep you from stumbling and to present you blameless before the presence of His glory with great joy, to the only God, our Savior, through Jesus Christ our Lord be glory, majesty, dominion, and authority, before all time and now and forever."*

Miracles and Worship
Luke 5

Memorize God's Word: Mark 1:17.

❖ Luke 5:1-11—Jesus Calls the First Disciples

1. What do you sense about the spiritual hunger of the people mentioned in verse 1?

   _____

   _____

2. What does the great catch of fish tell you about Jesus?

   _____

   _____

3. How would you explain Peter's reaction (verse 8)?

   _____

   _____

4. Have you ever felt as Peter does here or as the prophet did in Isaiah 6:5? Please explain.

   _____

   _____

5. What is the meaning of the phrase *"you will be catching men"* (5:10)?

   _____

   _____

❖ Luke 5:12-16—Jesus Heals a Leper

6. Read Mark 1:40-45; Leviticus 13:45-46.

     a. What do the leper's words, *"If You will, You can make me clean,"* tell you about his attitude about himself and his attitude toward Jesus?

        _____

        _____

     b. Jesus is able to heal with a word, yet He touches the leper. What does this tell you about His attitude toward this outcast of society?

        _____

        _____

7. What, besides the joy of being healed, do you think it means to this man to be touched by Jesus?

     _____

     _____

     _____

8. In verse 14, what do Jesus' instructions to the leper indicate about His attitude toward the Law?

     _____

     _____

❖ Luke 5:17-26—Jesus Heals a Paralytic

9. Who is present when Jesus heals the man who was paralyzed (5:17-19)?

     _____

     _____

10. How would you describe the paralyzed man's friends (5:18-20)?

     _____

     _____

11. As illustrated in this story, how would you define *faith*?

_____

_____

12. Why does Jesus first forgive the man's sin, when his obvious problem is a physical one?

_____

_____

13. What attitude do you sense in the Pharisees' questions (verse 21)?

_____

_____

14. How does Jesus define the real issue behind the Pharisees' questions (5:22-24) and how does He answer their questions?

_____

_____

❖ Luke 5:27-32—Jesus Calls Levi

15. Considering the type of business Levi (or Matthew, as he was known; Matthew 9:9-13) was in, what does this say about the kinds of people Jesus calls to follow Him?

_____

_____

16. What does this call imply about Levi's spiritual state?

_____

_____

17. The Pharisees see themselves as righteous men, not sinners (5:30). According to Romans 3:10-12, 22-23, what is their (and our) actual state?

_____

_____

_____

18. Who is the *"doctor"* Jesus refers to in Luke 5:31?

_____

19. In light of Romans 3:10, what does Jesus mean in verse 32?

_____

_____

❖ Luke 5:33-39—Jesus Talks About Fasting

20. How do the Pharisees view what makes a man truly spiritual (5:33)?

_____

_____

21. What is your understanding of the purpose of fasting? (See also Matthew 6:16-18.)

_____

_____

22. As illustrated in these parables, how do people generally react toward change?

_____

_____

Apply what you have learned. Jesus didn't flinch at upsetting traditions. He called simple fishermen rather than highly trained scholars to be His disciples. He graciously healed an "untouchable" leper. He not only healed a paralyzed man, but also forgave his sins. He ate a meal with tax collectors and sinners. He didn't require fasting when others thought He should. Traditions are not inherently bad, nor are they necessarily right. What traditions do you adhere to simply because they are traditions? Ask the Holy Spirit to help you examine your traditions in the light of Scripture and to help you adjust your beliefs and actions accordingly.

Miracles and Worship
Luke 5

Jesus Calls the Disciples

Chapter 5 begins with Jesus standing near the Lake of Gennesaret, also known as the Sea of Galilee. He is no stranger to some of the fishermen gathered there, including Andrew, Simon Peter, James, and John. Originally a follower of John the Baptist, Andrew follows Jesus after hearing John call Him *"the Lamb of God"* (John 1:36). Later he introduces Simon Peter to Jesus, saying, *"We have found the Messiah"* (1:41). Jesus tells these professional fishermen to *"put out into the deep and let down your nets for a catch"* (Luke 5:4). Having fished all night with no results, they may have questioned Him, but Simon Peter obeys. Imagine their amazement when the catch is so big they need help to load both boats!

Simon Peter and the other fishermen must have been amazed by the implications of what happened. Simon Peter knows Jesus' teaching is spiritual truth, but now he begins to understand Jesus' deity and see Him as Lord and master of the physical world. As Jews, Simon Peter and the others viewed God as so holy they wouldn't even pronounce His name. No wonder Simon Peter falls at Jesus' knees and confesses his sinfulness. Jesus, however, puts Peter's fears to rest and warmly welcomes his fellowship. His reply, *"Do not be afraid"* (5:10), echoes the angel Gabriel's words to Zechariah and the shepherds. We, too, can have that same fellowship with Jesus, but we must remember that it is a relationship of disciple and Lord.

Jesus Heals the Sick

In Jesus' day, Jews considered lepers physically and spiritually unclean and shunned them. Yet when a leper begs for healing, Jesus does so with a touch that heals him physically, spiritually, and emotionally. The leper knows Jesus can heal, but doubts that He will have anything to do with him. Jesus, as He often does, surprises him. He tells him not to speak of his healing but to go to the priest to be examined, then to thank God for his restored life by offering the prescribed sacrifice. But the news spreads, and many come to Jesus for healing.

Think about how Jesus could have healed the man with a word, yet He physically touched him—a simple act that surely washed away years of loneliness and self-hatred. To some degree, we can all relate to that man with leprosy. We too need God's healing touch to rid us of our diseases, physical and spiritual.

On Jesus' return to Capernaum, so many gather to hear Him that when some men bring a paralyzed friend to be healed, they cannot enter the house. Still determined, they climb to the rooftop and lower their friend through the tiles and into the crowd. Seeing their faith, Jesus addresses the man's primary need, saying, *"Man, your sins are forgiven you"* (5:20).

The Pharisees and teachers of the Law think Jesus is blaspheming and inwardly challenge His authority to forgive. The Pharisees loved to quote authorities. But Jesus' authority comes from God alone, and He says only what His Father wants Him to say (John 8:28). As a result, His teachings conflict with much of theirs, further setting them against Him. Knowing their thoughts, Jesus asks which is easier—to heal or to forgive. Then He proves His authority by healing the man, who gets up and goes home, praising God.

Jesus and the Tax Collectors

In Jesus' day, the Roman government placed a monetary value on a conquered region and sold it to the highest bidder, who—with the help of tax collectors—collected high taxes from the people. Tax collectors (publicans), among the most hated people in Israel, were Jews but were regarded as ceremonially unclean because they had frequent contact with Gentiles and willingly served the Romans.

When Jesus calls Levi, better known as Matthew, to follow Him, he instantly obeys, leaving everything to follow Jesus. Later he hosts a dinner in Jesus' honor—an ideal way to introduce fellow tax collectors to the Savior.

Questioning why Jesus and His disciples would eat with sinners, the Pharisees complain to the disciples rather than asking Jesus directly. Jesus' response reveals that He cannot help people like the Pharisees until they see their need of the salvation He offers them.

The Pharisees Question Jesus About Fasting

Devout Jews fasted and prayed regularly in expectation of the Messiah's coming. Contrary to this tradition, Jesus does not tell His disciples to fast. The reason is clear: The long-awaited Messiah is already present, so why fast?

Jesus uses two parables to explain His point. In the first, the new coat represents His message and teaching. The old coat symbolizes old religious habits and traditions. No one can take part of the new message and try to work it into the old without ruining the truth of both. In the second parable, He points out the uselessness of pouring new wine into an old wineskin. As it ferments, new wine expands and will burst a hardened old wineskin; both the wine and its container will be ruined. New wine was always poured into a new wineskin. The gospel message, represented by the new wine, must be contained in a new wineskin—an open heart and mind.

Jesus knows how some Jews will view the changes He is bringing. He concludes the parable with a proverb common in that day: *"The old is good"* (Luke 5:39). Some are comfortable with life as it is. They are set in their ways, and their minds are made up. John the Baptist came to prepare the way for a new era, but to live a life pleasing to God in this new time requires that people repent and change. The Pharisees' prejudice against Jesus keeps them from seeing the truth. Because of their narrow, inflexible outlook, they do not recognize Jesus as God's Son, the promised Messiah for whom they are waiting.

God has many ways to communicate the living, powerful gospel message to the human heart and mind. It is vital that we who believe be open to the truth of God's Word and sensitive to the Holy Spirit's prompting.

Personalize this lesson.

✓ "They [Pharisees] *said to Him* [Jesus], *'The disciples of John fast often and offer prayers, and so do the disciples of the Pharisees, but yours eat and drink'"* (Luke 5:33). The Pharisees' traditions told them that religious people should be pious and austere. But Jesus' disciples *"eat and drink"*; Jesus even ate and drank *"with tax collectors and sinners."* Did you—or does someone you know—assume that Christians are supposed to be perpetually long-faced and gloomy as they endure a somber life while hoping that all will be better in heaven? Well, all will be better in heaven, but life doesn't need to be merely endured now. Take some time to meditate on these verses: *"I came that they may have life and have it abundantly"* (John 10:10) and *"These things I have spoken to you, that My joy may be in you, and that your joy may be full"* (John 15:11). Talk to God about what it might look like to experience more life and joy in Him. He wants that for you—that's why He came.

Sowing and Reaping
Luke 6

Memorize God's Word: Luke 6:38.

❖ Luke 6:1-16—The Lord of the Sabbath

1. Why do the Pharisees say it is unlawful for the disciples to pick and eat grain on the Sabbath (6:2; See also Deuteronomy 23:25)?

   _____

   _____

2. What was God's original purpose in giving man the Sabbath? (See Exodus 23:12.)

   _____

   _____

3. Read Mark 2:27. What does Jesus mean when He says that *"the Sabbath was made for man"* (See also Exodus 20:11.)

   _____

   _____

   _____

4. Are Christians under the Mosaic Sabbath Law? (See Romans 14:5; Colossians 2:16.)

   _____

   _____

   _____

5. How does Jesus choose the 12 apostles from all His other disciples?

_____

_____

❖ Luke 6:17-26—The Secret of Blessing

6. Read Matthew 5:3-12 and compare with the passage from Luke. How does Matthew's account differ from Luke's in his list of conditions that make one blessed?

_____

_____

7. In light of the different kinds of people we have seen Jesus encounter, who might the list of "woes" pertain to?

_____

_____

8. What is the main point Luke makes in verses 20-26?

_____

_____

9. How does this message relate to you?

_____

_____

❖ Luke 6:27-36—Love Your Enemies

10. How is it possible to follow the commands in verses 27-31? (See also John 14:15-17.)

_____

_____

11. What is the key verse in this passage and why?

_____

_____

12. In light of the fact that *"all have sinned"* (Romans 3:23), in what sense does Jesus use the word *"sinners"* (6:32)?

_____

_____

13. What is one term the New Testament uses for believers in Jesus? (See Romans 1:7.)

_____

_____

14. Considering your answers above and this passage in Luke, how is a believer to be different from an unbeliever?

_____

_____

❖ Luke 6:37-45—The Law of Return

15. Hypocrites pretend to be what they are not, or pretend to be better than they really are; they mask the truth. What might Jesus want to emphasize by using the words *"speck"* and *"log"* (6:41)?

_____

_____

16. What does the tree represent in a person's life? What is the fruit?

_____

_____

17. What are the two types of trees and how are their natures revealed?

_____

_____

18. How do people reveal their nature?

_____

_____

❖ Luke 6:46-49—How We Are to Build

19. Read Matthew 7:21-27. Compare Luke 6:46 with Matthew 7:21. How is a true follower of Christ revealed in the present and rewarded in the future?

_____

_____

20. Our lives, now and eternally, are the houses we build. Who is the rock on which our foundation is laid? (See also 1 Corinthians 3:11; 1 Peter 2:4-8.)

_____

_____

21. What do the words *"when a flood arose"* (6:48) tell you about life?

_____

_____

22. What does this passage indicate about the security we have in Christ?

_____

_____

Apply what you have learned. Do you ever try to protect yourself from change or trouble? Most of us do. We like to think we can control events to meet our desires. Yet we all reach the limit in how far we can truly control our lives. Jesus points to Himself as the source of inner strength for those of us who believe in Him. Though our circumstances may change, *"Jesus Christ is the same yesterday and today and forever"* (Hebrews 13:8). That truth is *"a sure and steadfast anchor of the soul"* (Hebrews 6:19). What circumstances are you trying to control? Will you release control to God and trust Him to work things out for you?

Sowing and Reaping
Luke 6

The Sabbath's True Meaning

When the disciples pluck and eat grain one Sabbath, they break the Law according to the religious traditionalists who have added countless rules to the Sabbath Law God gave Israel. The Pharisees care more about keeping rules than about the welfare of God's people. Forbidding 39 types of work on this sacred day, they judge plucking grain as reaping, rubbing their hands as threshing, and throwing away hulls as winnowing. Jesus reminds them of a similar situation faced by King David (1 Samuel 21:1-6), implying that David fed his men with something sacred to God, yet lawful for man to use for his good. God created the Sabbath for our benefit (Exodus 20:8-11; Mark 2:27). As God in the flesh, Jesus does not need to justify His actions, for He is *"Lord of the Sabbath"* (Luke 6:5).

Think about when Jesus asked, *"Have you not read… ?"* (6:3). Yes, of course they had read and could quote Scriptures word for word. But they had not understood what they read. It is possible for us to do the same—read the Bible faithfully, even memorize verses, and yet fail to understand its message. The Holy Spirit enables us to understand God's Word, but we must ask for His guidance. *"When the Spirit of truth comes, He will guide you into all the truth"* (John 16:13).

The religious officials *"watched Him … so that they might find a reason to accuse Him"* (Luke 6:7). Jesus knows this, but also knows how much the man with the shriveled hand has suffered. He asks His opponents, *"Is it lawful on the Sabbath to do good or to do harm, to save life or to destroy it?"* (6:9). No one replies, and Jesus heals the man. The officials are *"filled with fury and discussed with one another what they might do to Jesus"* (6:11). They follow the Law so exactly that they miss its true purpose.

The Chosen Apostles

Jesus prays all night before choosing 12 apostles from among His disciples. A disciple is an apprentice; an apostle is a chosen messenger with a specific mission. All those chosen have ordinary jobs. Peter, Andrew, James, and John are fishermen. Matthew, a tax collector employed by Rome, formerly helped cheat his fellow Jews, who consider him a traitor. Simon the zealot may belong to a group of Jewish radicals who use armed resistance against Rome. Although Jesus knows Judas Iscariot will betray Him (John 6:64), He still makes him an apostle. By making evil choices, Judas will later fulfill Jesus' description of him as a *"devil"* (6:70-71). Thomas is well-known for expressing doubts after the Resurrection, but later declares, *"my Lord and my God"* (20:28). Philip will become a great evangelist (Acts 8:26-40). Bartholomew, James the son of Alphaeus, and Judas the son of James complete the group.

The Guide for Successful Living

In the *beatitudes* (Latin, *blessed*), Jesus states the rewards waiting for those who please God. Unlike Matthew's parallel record (Matthew 5:1-12), Luke's account also gives related woes for those who will face judgment.

In the first beatitude, Jesus blesses the poor and confronts our tendency to pursue riches. When Jesus says, *"Blessed are you who are hungry now, for you shall be satisfied"* (Luke 6:21), He is referring to those who long for righteousness (Matthew 5:6). In contrast, the *"full"* (Luke 6:25) will be left wanting on God's Judgment Day. People who suffer through trials are promised a future joy, while those who pursue pleasure in this life—never giving a thought to spiritual matters—*"shall mourn and weep"* (6:25), recognizing their poverty too late. Jesus tells those who endure persecution and rejection for Him to *"rejoice … your reward is great in heaven"* (6:23).

Love Your Enemies

In the context of loving one's enemies, Jesus speaks of *agape* (unconditional) love. Because such love is a gift from God (1 Corinthians 13), it does not fail. *Agape* love enables us to do good to those who hate us, bless those who curse us, and pray for those who mistreat us. Agape love is an act of the will, not a feeling. Although we may not *feel* kind or patient, we can still express kindness and patience to others. We can choose our own attitudes and actions. Jesus told His disciples to love one another (John 15:12). He would not command the impossible; if He told us to love others, then with the Holy Spirit's help we can do so.

Judging Others

God is the final judge of all people. By His grace believers' sins are forgiven and we escape His righteous judgments. He expects us to show a similarly gracious attitude to others. If you show mercy, God will be merciful to you. If you give to others, it will be given to you in *"good measure, pressed down"* (Luke 6:38). This refers to the way merchants sold grain; they put it into a sack and shook it down so more could be poured in.

Jesus warns us to be careful about whom we follow. If a teacher is spiritually blind, the student will be, too, and both will fall. Jesus uses the word *speck* to describe another's fault and the word *log* to describe our own. People with critical spirits see others' failings as larger than they are and their own shortcomings as smaller. We must deal first with our own faults before gently confronting those of others. Jesus did not come to condemn (John 3:17), and we should follow His example.

Good and Bad Fruit

Any plant's fruit or flower is the natural product of that plant's inner life. The fruit is always true to the plant's nature. This is true in our lives as well. Despite attempts to appear different from what we are, our true nature will eventually come out.

Finally, Jesus warns that those who call Him *"Lord"* (Luke 6:46) but do not obey Him are like people who build a house with no foundation. When a flood comes, the house collapses. On the other hand, those who put His words into practice are safe when the floods of trouble come. Jesus Christ is the one and only foundation, *"the Rock of our salvation"* (Psalm 95:1).

Personalize this lesson.

☑ Do you feel poor, hungry, sad, excluded, reviled, or spurned in any way? Pour out your heart to God. Thank Him that even in this condition, He welcomes, loves, and blesses you. Ask Him to help you see some of those blessings. Write down anything He reveals to you.

Trust and Forgiveness
Luke 7

❖ Luke 7:1-10—The Centurion's Faith

1. What is the centurion's association with the Jewish people, and what has he done for them?

   _____

   _____

2. The centurion says he lives under authority and is also in authority over others. How does he apply that to Jesus?

   _____

   _____

   _____

3. What about the centurion amazes Jesus?

   _____

   _____

   _____

❖ Luke 7:11-17—The Widow's Son

4. Does the widow of Nain ask Jesus to help her? In fact, does the account indicate any faith on her part?

   _____

   _____

   _____

5. What is the determining factor in Jesus' decision to raise the young man to life?

_____

_____

6. What proof does Luke offer that this miracle was real?

_____

_____

7. What does this event tell you about Jesus' power over death?

_____

_____

❖ Luke 7:18-23—Jesus and John the Baptist

8. John was filled with the Holy Spirit and testified about Jesus. Why does he send two disciples to Him with the question seen in verse 19?

_____

_____

_____

9. Why do you think Jesus answers as He does in verse 22? (See Isaiah 35:4-6; 61:1.)

_____

_____

10. Do John's actions and questions encourage or discourage you? Why?

_____

_____

11. When are we likely to question who Jesus is and what He is doing?

_____

_____

12. What is the difference between unbelief and doubt?

_____

_____

❖ Luke 7:24-35—Jesus Validates John's Ministry

13. What do you think Jesus means by His questions in verses 24-25? (See also Matthew 3:1-4.)

_____

_____

_____

14. Why does Jesus call John *"more than a prophet"* (7:26)? (See also Malachi 3:1.)

_____

_____

15. What is Jesus saying about the people (Luke 7:31-34)?

_____

_____

❖ Luke 7:36-50—Perfume and Repentance

16. How would you describe the woman and her *actions* (7:37-38)?

_____

_____

17. How would you describe Simon the Pharisee's *attitude* (7:39)?

_____

_____

18. Why do you think Jesus initiates the conversation with Simon by using a parable (7:40-43)?

_____

_____

19. What do Jesus' words in verses 44-46 tell you about Simon? About the woman?

_____

_____

20. What is Jesus saying about sin and forgiveness (7:47)?

_____

_____

21. How should Jesus' words (7:47) affect Simon's opinion of himself and his view of sin?

_____

_____

22. How would you apply these words to your life?

_____

_____

_____

_____

Apply what you have learned. Luke records two miracles—first the healing of the centurion's servant, then the even more spectacular resurrection of a widow's only son. Then, before moving on to record Jesus' declaration of forgiveness of a woman's sins, Luke inserts John the Baptist's question—via his disciples— about Jesus' identity: *"Are you the one who is to come, or shall we look for another?"* (7:20). Why this order? Is it simple chronology? Could it be that Luke placed this record here to suggest to his readers that we too, like John the Baptist, need to work through what we believe about Jesus? Jesus didn't reprimand His cousin for his doubts. He simply told him to consider the evidence, the miracles. If doubts strike you, consider the evidence—it's all there.

Trust and Forgiveness
Luke 7

Jesus Heals and Resurrects

As Jesus enters Capernaum, some Jewish elders bring Him a request from a Roman centurion whose servant is dying. Romans and Jews generally despised each other, but the elders' pleadings imply that this centurion is different. Roman law viewed slaves as "living tools," yet the centurion cares about his slave. His request, seen in verses 6-7, reveals his humility and thoughtfulness. Knowing that Jews do not enter Gentile homes, he spares Jesus the awkwardness of coming into his house.

As an officer, the centurion understands authority. He believes Jesus is under God's authority, but also has authority over His creation. The centurion comprehends what many Jews cannot when Jesus says, *"The words that I say to you I do not speak on My own authority, but the Father who dwells in Me does His works"* (John 14:10). Jesus marvels at this Gentile and honors him for having a faith greater than that of the Israelites. He does not touch—or even see—the slave, but says, *"Go; let it be done for you as you have believed"* (Matthew 8:13). What a demonstration of the power of His Word.

As Jesus, His disciples, and followers arrive at Nain, a widow's only son is about to be buried. Moved by her grief, Jesus touches the coffin and tells the dead man to get up. He sits up and speaks. The awed crowd praises God and spreads this news about Jesus.

Jesus and John the Baptist

In prison, John the Baptist hears of the events in Capernaum and Nain. He sends his disciples to ask Jesus, *"Are You the one who is to come, or shall we look for another?"* (Luke 7:20). Coming from the one who pointed to Jesus as the Messiah, this is a surprising question. The Bible makes it clear that God's servants are not perfect; they have doubts and fears, as we all do. As proof that He is the promised Messiah, Jesus tells John's disciples to *"tell John what you have seen and heard: the blind receive their sight, the lame walk, lepers are cleansed, and the deaf hear, the dead are raised up, the poor have good news preached to them"* (7:22).

Think about how John the Baptist went directly to Jesus for answers to his doubts. When we have doubts about Christ, do we go to Him with our questions? Like John the Baptist, go to the Source for answers. If we sincerely ask for His truth, He will reveal it to us (Luke 11:9; James 1:5).

In spite of criticism and persecution, John is faithful in his task to the end. He has chosen a simple and sacrificial life, wholly dedicated to God. Jesus does not criticize John for his doubts—He praises him for faithfully furthering God's kingdom on earth.

Jesus says John the Baptist is greater than any man who ever lived. His ministry closes the time of the Old Testament prophets and ushers in the time of the New Testament, which will be fully established by Jesus' death and resurrection. John acts as a bridge between the two periods and has the unique privilege of introducing the Messiah to Israel. He remains the greatest of all the prophets, but his greatness cannot be compared to those who have the blessings and benefits of God's new covenant era. In terms of privileges, even the least in God's kingdom is more blessed than John the Baptist.

Luke compares two groups who have heard John's message. First is the general public, including the outcasts and oppressed. John had baptized these people and they *"declared God just"* (Luke 7:29). Second are the religious elite, who fail to see their need to repent. They refuse John's baptism and have *"rejected the purpose of God"* (7:30). Society's outcasts respond more enthusiastically to God's righteous demands than do the spiritual leaders of that day. Jesus compares those who reject Him to children who refuse to be pleased with anything. They criticize John for his austerity and then criticize Jesus for His lack of austerity. In the end, Jesus says God's wisdom will be proven by His children—through the evidence of the changed lives of those who love and obey Him.

Perfume and Repentance

When Simon the Pharisee invites Jesus to dinner, Jesus goes to his house and reclines at the table. It was the custom for a host's servant to wash a guest's feet and provide ointment for his head. Simon neglects both of these courtesies, showing his lack of regard for his guest. Apparently, he wants only to interrogate Him. Meals were often eaten in an open courtyard, allowing the eager public to gather and listen to a visiting rabbi. An outsider could easily enter the courtyard and approach a guest, which explains how a *"sinner,"* perhaps a prostitute, has access to Jesus.

What courage it takes for her to approach Jesus. As she stands behind Him, she begins to weep. She wets His feet with her tears and dries them with her hair. Then, she kisses His feet and anoints them with costly perfume. This woman gives Jesus something she treasures—probably the only thing of value she has. The Pharisee wonders if Jesus is truly a prophet, assuming He would not allow such a woman to touch Him. Knowing Simon's thoughts, Jesus tells a story about two people who owe money: one borrowed a small amount of money and the other a much larger amount. When neither could repay him, the lender canceled both debts. Jesus asks, *"Now which of them will love him more?"* Simon rightly replies, *"The one … for whom he cancelled the larger debt"* (7:42-43). Simon's answer establishes Jesus' point. Jesus then contrasts the woman's loving behavior toward Him with Simon's disregard.

Jesus concludes, *"Her sins, which are many, are forgiven—for she loved much. But he who is forgiven little, loves little"* (7:47). Her salvation is a result of her faith. She responds to God in love because her many sins are forgiven.

Personalize this lesson.

☑ Simon, a Pharisee, assumed he was a good man, doing Jesus a favor in inviting Him to his home for a meal. He seemed oblivious to any needs he personally may have had. Meanwhile, the unnamed sinner woman who showed up at the meal had no trouble understanding the extent of her need. She admitted her guilt and shame, accepted the gift of forgiveness, and then openly displayed her gratitude. Her guilt and shame were actually gifts, too, because they pointed her toward her need of Jesus' forgiveness. Simon, on the other hand, was too proud to feel guilt and shame, so he saw no need to be forgiven. Have you ever thought of guilt and shame as gifts? If guilt and shame have led you to repentance, take some time to thank God for using them as gifts in your life. Don't get stuck in shame and guilt, though. Let them become catalysts that lead you to the freedom that comes through repentance and forgiveness (see 1 John 1:9). If you have never felt guilt and shame, ask God to show you whether that's because you've never sinned or because you've been too proud to see your sin and your need of a Savior.

Lesson 10

Receiving and Obeying
Luke 8:1-21

Memorize God's Word: Matthew 5:16.

❖ Luke 8:1-3—Women Follow Jesus

1. What do the women mentioned in verses 2-3 have in common?

_____

_____

_____

_____

2. If we imitated these women, what would our response to Jesus look like?

_____

_____

_____

❖ Luke 8:4-15—The Parable of the Sower

3. In what way is the seed like the Word of God?

_____

_____

4. What happens to the seed sown among thorns?

_____

_____

5. How would you describe the cares, riches, or pleasures that could be thorns in a person's life?

    _____

    _____

6. What parallel do you see in the John 15:1-5 passage to the parable of the sower?

    _____

    _____

    _____

❖ Luke 8:16-18—The Parable of the Lamp

7. From whom do believers receive their light? (See John 8:12.)

    _____

    _____

8. According to this parable, what is the purpose of our lives?

    _____

    _____

9. Reread Luke 8:16-18. (See also Matthew 25:14-30.)

    a. Does this warning involve only what and how we hear? Explain.

        _____

        _____

    b. What are the implications concerning how one uses or neglects the light God gives?

        _____

        _____

    c. What are examples of how this is true in other areas of life?

        _____

        _____

        _____

❖ Luke 8:19-21—Family and Spiritual Kin

10. What kind of person does Jesus consider a part of His spiritual family? (See also Matthew 12:46-50.)

_____

_____

11. How should members of God's family relate to one another in light of Jesus' comparison between natural family relationships and that of believers?

_____

_____

_____

12. What are examples of how we can better relate to those in God's family?

_____

_____

_____

13. Read James 1:22-25. What are the characteristics of a person who hears but does not obey God's Word?

_____

_____

14. From the parable in verses 11-15, what type of soil do you think describes this person?

_____

_____

15. What does the phrase *"he will be blessed in his doing"* (James 1:25) convey to you about what we receive when we obey?

_____

_____

_____

❖ Luke 8:1-21—Review

16. How does the title "Receiving and Obeying" apply to this lesson?

_____

_____

_____

17. What other titles might be appropriate?

_____

_____

18. Briefly summarize the main message of this lesson in two or three sentences.

_____

_____

_____

Apply what you have learned. Jesus said that those who apply the truth of the light given will be given more light—but those who ignore or neglect the light not only fail to get more but will lose what they already have. Think about that principle played out to the fullest extent. Jude says that those who have *"abandoned themselves for the sake of gain"* are destined for *"the gloom of utter darkness"* (Jude 11; 13). Meanwhile, Revelation 22:5, referring to the new heaven and new earth, says, *"Night will be no more. They will need no light of lamp or sun, for the Lord God will be their light, and they will reign forever and ever."* Have you thanked God for the light He has given you? How are you using that light for His Kingdom?

Receiving and Obeying
Luke 8:1-21

Women were not highly regarded in Jesus' day, although they fared better in the Jewish culture than in the Gentile world. But Luke's Gospel gives women special honor. Luke showed Jesus' compassion for a grieving mother (7:12-15) and a sinful woman (7:36-50). Now he gives an account, found only in this Gospel, of Mary Magdalene, Joanna, and Susanna.

Women Follow Jesus

Jesus came to *"preach the good news of the kingdom of God"* (4:43), but opposition from religious officials grows so severe He can no longer speak in synagogues. He now travels through towns and villages *"proclaiming and bringing the good news of the kingdom of God"* (8:1). As He preaches in the Galilean countryside, His disciples help Him, and godly women support Him. By accepting their support and allowing them to minister to Him, Jesus affirms their personal worth and the value of their contribution to God's work.

Some people think Mary Magdalene was the *"sinner"* mentioned in 7:37, although Scripture does not state this. She was *"healed of evil spirits and infirmities"* (8:2) and now faithfully follows and supports the One who set her free. Evidence of her loyalty includes her presence at Jesus' crucifixion (John 19:25) and His burial (Matthew 27:61). Most significantly, she is the first person to see the risen Christ (John 20:11-18).

Joanna, wife of Chuza, manager and financial officer of Herod the tetrarch's household, was likely a member of the upper class. We don't know how she suffered or how Jesus healed her. However, her encounter with Him is so meaningful that she aids Him in spite of her husband's close association with Herod. Her presence at Jesus' crucifixion and her preparation of spices for His burial show her devotion to Him (Luke 24:1, 9-10). Susanna is mentioned by name only in verse 3. We know nothing about her except that she, too, follows the Lord and assists Him from her own resources.

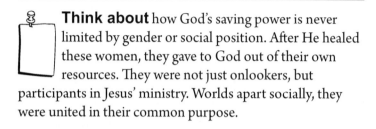

Think about how God's saving power is never limited by gender or social position. After He healed these women, they gave to God out of their own resources. They were not just onlookers, but participants in Jesus' ministry. Worlds apart socially, they were united in their common purpose.

Jesus Speaks in Parables

Jesus often taught in parables (stories from nature or daily life that hold a hidden truth). Those whose hearts were open to God were more likely to understand the deeper meaning, but hardhearted people were confused. Jesus taught the crowd about the sower and the seed. Seed that fell along a path was exposed to trampling and to birds and had no chance to grow. Seed that fell on rock did not develop deep roots, so could not survive. Seed sown among weeds began to grow, but was soon choked. The seed in good soil had all the right conditions for growth, producing a crop 100 times larger than what had been sown.

Later, Jesus explains this parable to His disciples (Mark 4:10-20). The seed is the Word of God *"living and active"* (Hebrews 4:12). A crop's success depends on seed taking root properly in good soil. The soil represents hearts. Seed lying on the path symbolizes people who hear God's Word, but have such hard attitudes it never penetrates their hearts. The evil one snatches God's Truth away. Seed that lands on rock represents those who hear the Word and get excited about it, but because they do not obey it, the Word does not take root in their hearts. When tested or tried, their faith withers and they fall back into their old ways. The seed that falls among thorns represents those who hear and believe God's Word. Yet life's troubles or pleasures soon choke this seed. The rich young ruler (Mark 10:21-23) and Demas, who deserted Paul (2 Timothy 4:10), are examples of seed that fell among thorns. Seed that falls on good soil represents those who faithfully cultivate what God has sown in their lives. They hear God's message, remember it, obey, and produce a life rich in godly character.

After the parable of the sower, Jesus discusses three truths. First, He illustrates what a believer's life should look like. Jesus calls Himself and believers *"the light of the world"* (John 8:12; Matthew 5:14). We who believe in Christ receive His light (His truth) and reflect it to others by our godly behavior. People watch to see if our talk matches our walk.

Second, Jesus explains that our true selves will be revealed. We try to hide sin in our hearts, from God, others, and even ourselves. We may not see our need to change. However, as we turn our life over to Christ, He begins to make us more like Himself. He gives us a new heart and fills us with His Spirit, renewing us as we study and obey His Word.

The third truth warns us to listen carefully. When we act on truth, we receive more truth—but when we ignore it, even what we received is taken away. Abilities put to use grow more effective, while neglected ones often fade. Being obedient to the light we have ensures we are given more light; disobedience leads to darkness.

True Kinship

Jesus warned that a person's enemies might be from his or her own household (Matthew 10:36). Members of Jesus' family sometimes hindered His ministry. Once, they intended to interrupt His teaching because they thought He was out of His mind (Mark 3:21). At another point in His ministry, they did not believe in Him and tried to pressure Him into a dangerous situation (John 7:1-5).

Verses 19-21 show Him teaching about God's family. The Holy Spirit lives in those who have faith in Christ, and they become members of God's eternal family—a family not limited by the natural family structure. God created the natural family, so Jesus is not saying the family is bad or unnecessary. Jesus loved His family. But, like everything in our fallen world, family does not always fulfill the full potential God intended. God's family, on the other hand, is the ideal of which the natural family is only a shadow.

Personalize this lesson.

☑ The parable of the sower describes different kinds of soil, symbolizing the many responses people have to the gospel. The quality of our life of faith is greatly affected by how we respond to the truth we are given. Jesus said we are responsible to use it wisely. We must not let our hearts become hard, shallow, or choked by distractions. No matter how we began, we can change—if we pay attention to spiritual truth. List some ways that paying attention to spiritual truth is changing you.

Dominion and Power
Luke 8:22-56

❖ Luke 8:22-25—Jesus Calms the Storm

1. How would you describe the positive and negative elements in the disciples' words to Jesus (8:24)?

_____

_____

_____

2. Have you ever cried out to Jesus as the disciples did? (See Mark 4:35-41.) If so, how did Jesus encourage you?

_____

_____

_____

3. Knowing there would be a storm, Jesus still initiates the boat trip across the lake. What does this tell you about following Jesus?

_____

_____

❖ Luke 8:26-33—Deliverance From Demons

4. What is afflicting this man? (See also Mark 5:2.)

_____

_____

_____

5. How would you describe his appearance and where he lives?

_____

_____

_____

6. How does he show unusual strength?

_____

_____

7. What is his emotional and mental state? (See also Mark 5:5.)

_____

_____

8. What implications do you draw from the demons' recognition of Jesus?

_____

_____

_____

9. What does the number of demons in this man tell you about the nature of evil?

_____

_____

❖ Luke 8:34-39—The Healing Brings Results

10. What changes do the people find when they come to see this man?

_____

_____

_____

11. Why do you think the people were afraid?

_____

_____

12. Do people react similarly to Jesus today? Explain your answer.

_____

_____

13. a. Jesus sends the healed man home to tell everyone how much
        God has done for him. How would the people in that area
        benefit?

    _____

    _____

    b. How does your answer above affect your understanding of
        your privilege as a believer in Christ?

    _____

    _____

❖ Luke 8:40-48—A Sick Woman's Faith

14. How would you describe the difference in attitude between the
    Gerasenes Jesus had just left and the people seen in verse 40?

    _____

    _____

15. How would you describe the faith of the woman who touches
    Jesus' cloak? (See Mark 5:25-34.)

    _____

    _____

16. What do you think the woman might have been thinking or
    feeling as she approached Jesus?

    _____

    _____

17. How might Jesus' acceptance of this woman encourage someone
    who feels unworthy to approach God?

    _____

    _____

❖ Luke 8:49-56—Jairus and His Daughter

18. How might Jairus have reacted to the report of his daughter's death, or to Jesus saying, *"Do not fear; only believe, and she will be well"* (8:50)? (See also Mark 5:21-23, 35-43.)

_____

_____

19. Have you ever had to choose between believing Jesus or believing circumstances? Explain your answer.

_____

_____

20. Why do the mourners laugh at Jesus' explanation that the girl is sleeping?

_____

_____

21. Why does Jesus command that the girl be given something to eat?

_____

_____

Apply what you have learned. Jairus's daughter was restored to life when Jesus caused her spirit to return to her body (Luke 8:55). Similarly, we are restored to newness of life through our faith in Jesus Christ. Through His Spirit we receive the breath of new, everlasting life. What principles about trusting Jesus through trials, or about new life, have you learned from this lesson, and how, specifically, will you apply these principles in your life?

Dominion and Power
Luke 8:22-56

Jesus Calms the Storm

Jesus regularly teaches people from a boat offshore, which is perhaps why He is found near the Sea of Galilee in this account. As He and the disciples sail across the lake, Jesus falls asleep. Known for its sudden storms, the sea begins to rage.

The disciples—fishermen who know how to handle a boat in stormy weather—wake Jesus, fearing for their lives. He rebukes the wind and water, ending the storm. Waves usually remain rough for hours after a storm, but here the sea is calm. Awed, the disciples ask, *"Who then is this? … even winds and water … obey Him"* (Luke 8:25).

The disciples' fear shows that they lack faith in their own abilities, but neither do they trust Jesus. They have seen Him perform miracles, but they fail to recognize that true safety comes from being with Him—regardless of circumstances.

Think about two essential qualities of Jesus: His total humanity and His total deity. Jesus experiences human hunger and exhaustion, yet the winds and waves obey Him. He controls all nature because He created it (Colossians 1:16-17). Have you, just like the disciples, asked, "Who is Jesus?" Although He is fully God, He came to earth as a man to identify with you and take away your sin. This God-man wants to have a personal relationship with you.

Jesus initiated the trip across the sea (Luke 8:22; Matthew 8:23; Mark 4:35), and He did not promise the disciples an easy voyage. He allows troubles into believers' lives as well. Sometimes He removes our raging storm; at other times, He gives us grace to endure it (John 16:33).

Deliverance From Demons

In the region of the Gerasenes, a demon-possessed man confronts Jesus. Moved with compassion, Jesus commands the demon to leave. The demon responds, *"What have You to do with me, Jesus, Son of the Most High God? I beg You, do not torment me"* (Luke 8:28). Satan's agents shudder at the presence of the one true God (James 2:19). The *"many demons"* (Luke 8:30) beg Jesus not to cast them into the Abyss. They ask instead to enter a herd of pigs. Jesus allows them to go, and the demons cause the pigs to stampede into the sea. When the people from the town come to investigate, they find the healed man sitting at Jesus' feet. Afraid and probably angry at the loss of income, they ask Jesus to leave. The healed man begs to follow Him, but Jesus sends him home to share what God has done for him. On another occasion, Jesus tells a man cleansed of leprosy not to tell anyone (5:14). Jesus comprehends every situation and tailors His guidance according to what people truly need.

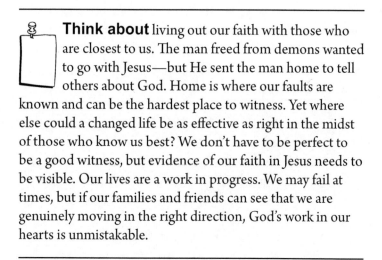

Think about living out our faith with those who are closest to us. The man freed from demons wanted to go with Jesus—but He sent the man home to tell others about God. Home is where our faults are known and can be the hardest place to witness. Yet where else could a changed life be as effective as right in the midst of those who know us best? We don't have to be perfect to be a good witness, but evidence of our faith in Jesus needs to be visible. Our lives are a work in progress. We may fail at times, but if our families and friends can see that we are genuinely moving in the right direction, God's work in our hearts is unmistakable.

Human Needs Collide

Jesus never refuses to help anyone who asks for His aid. Whether it is a great teacher of Israel (John 3:1-10), a Roman centurion (Luke 7:1-8), a child (Matthew 19:13-15), or a woman condemned by others (John 8:1-11), His response is loving and compassionate. His response to us is the same today as it was then: *"Come to Me, all who labor and are heavy laden, and I will give you rest"* (Matthew 11:28).

Jesus and His disciples return to Galilee, where a crowd awaits them. Jairus, a synagogue ruler, begs Jesus to heal his dying child. Walking through the crowd, Jesus recognizes a touch of faith as distinct from the jostling crowd. A woman who has suffered from a bleeding condition confesses and explains that merely touching Jesus has healed her. Her illness had caused her to be both ceremonially unclean and a social outcast. Jesus' response confirms her physical healing and her restoration to society. Meanwhile, someone arrives to say Jairus' daughter has died. Despite this news, Jesus reassures Jairus that He will heal his daughter. Jairus chooses to believe Jesus rather than his friend's report.

At Jairus's home, Jesus tells the mourners, *"Do not weep, for she is not dead but sleeping"* (8:52). They laugh at Him. Matthew 9:25 states, *"When the crowd had been put outside, He went in."* Perhaps the mourners are led outside because of their mocking disbelief. Jesus enters the home with the girl's parents and three of His disciples. He speaks to the girl as though she is just asleep, and the girl's spirit returns. She is alive! Jesus tells her parents to feed her and orders them not to tell anyone what has happened. Despite Jesus' request, news of the miracle spreads throughout the region.

Other than the girl's parents, Jesus asks only Peter, James, and John to enter Jairus's home. He undoubtedly has a reason for taking these men. They would later be with Him for significant occasions including the Transfiguration (Luke 9:28) and prayer at the Garden of Gethsemane (Mark 14:33). Jesus is preparing them for important responsibilities in the future. Peter will become a powerful speaker (Acts 2:14-41), one of the pillars of the first church and writer of two New Testament letters. James, John's brother, will be the first martyr among Christ's disciples (Acts 12:2). John, *"one of His disciples, whom Jesus loved"* (John 13:23), will write the books bearing his name (his Gospel and three letters found in the New Testament), as well as the book of Revelation. Peter, James, and John are three ordinary men who spend time with Jesus and find their lives changed forever.

Personalize this lesson.

✓ How could a few men in a fishing boat overcome the danger of a violent storm? The disciples were absolutely hopeless—until Jesus intervened. The demon-possessed man could not be controlled or cleansed of his evil spirits. He was absolutely hopeless— until Jesus intervened. The woman had suffered with bleeding for 12 years; her health and wealth were gone. She was absolutely hopeless— until Jesus intervened. Jairus's daughter had died. Jairus was absolutely hopeless—until.

Jesus intervened when these people were hopeless and helpless. He doesn't intervene for people who are confident of their own abilities to "fix" themselves. Like a wise lifeguard, He waits for the drowning person to quit flailing before He carries him safely to shore. In what areas of your life do you need to admit your helplessness and ask for His help?

Mission: Its Call and Cost
Luke 9:1-27

Memorize God's Word: Luke 9:23.

❖ Luke 9:1-6—Jesus Commissions the Twelve

1. Jesus is the source of the disciples' authority. What does He tell them to do?

   _____

   _____

2. What do you see that shows Jesus' concern for the whole person?

   _____

   _____

3. What do verses 1-2 imply for our ministry in the world today? (See also John 14:12-14.)

   _____

   _____

❖ Luke 9:7-9—Herod's Confusion

4. Read Mark 6:14-29. How would you describe Herod?

   _____

   _____

5. How did Herod react to John the Baptist? (See also Mark 6:20.)

   _____

   _____

6. What attitude does Herod depict? (See also Mark 6:26.)

_____

7. From Luke 9:7-9, why does Herod want to see Jesus?

_____

_____

❖ Luke 9:10-17—Jesus Feeds the Five Thousand

8. How do the disciples provide a model for accountability in Christian service (9:10)?

_____

_____

9. What do you think Mark 6:31-34 is saying about priorities?

_____

_____

10. In light of this example of spiritual priorities, what changes might be necessary in your schedule?

_____

_____

11. Why does Jesus encourage His disciples to take responsibility for feeding the people? (See also Mark 6:30-44.)

_____

_____

12. What practical solution to the problem do the disciples propose?

_____

_____

13. How does Jesus' response to their suggestion encourage you?

_____

_____

_____

❖ Luke 9:18-22—Peter Confesses Jesus' Identity

14. Peter says Jesus is the Christ (9:20; see also Matthew 16:16). How does he know who Jesus really is? (See Matthew 16:13-17.)

_____

_____

15. From what source do we get *our* convictions about who Jesus is? (See John 16:13-14.)

_____

_____

16. Who is Jesus to you?

_____

_____

_____

_____

17. Why is this the wrong time for the disciples to publicly proclaim Jesus' true identity?

_____

_____

18. What might the consequences be for believers today who proclaim His true identity?

_____

_____

_____

❖ Luke 9:23-27—Denying Ourselves

19. How are we to deny ourselves?

_____

_____

_____

20. In what ways can we daily take up our cross?

_____

_____

_____

21. What do you think verses 24-25 mean?

_____

_____

22. What social pressures today might cause a believer to hesitate in proclaiming Jesus Christ or living for Him?

_____

_____

_____

_____

Apply what you have learned. What does it mean to deny myself? Does it mean losing my personality? Does it mean losing the distinctives that make me who I am? No, it means putting God's will and the needs of my neighbor ahead of my desires. It means traveling the narrow road (Matthew 7:13). But it also means denying my desire to make my own way, to be self-sufficient—it means trusting Him rather than myself. In what areas do you need to set aside your desires for self-sufficiency and personal gain and follow Jesus down the narrow road?

Mission: Its Call and Cost
Luke 9:1-27

The Disciples' First Mission

Jesus commissions the Twelve to carry on His healing and preaching ministry so that many will believe in Him and be saved. Knowing He will not be with them much longer, He sends His disciples out in pairs (Mark 6:7) to begin their ministry and to prepare for greater tasks, such as casting out demons or healing diseases. He gives His disciples power and authority—key elements in the gospel ministry.

Jesus gives His disciples authority over demons, as well as power to heal physical diseases. Jesus knew that those who suffered due to demons or illness needed most of all to be reconciled to God; therefore, *"He sent them out to preach the kingdom of God"* (Luke 9:2). His disciples (then and now) are to minister to the whole person.

Jesus tells His disciples to take nothing with them and to trust God for everything, including material needs. More importantly, God provides the power and authority to complete their tasks. Their faith will grow as they depend on God's grace and hospitality from others. Jesus instructs them to stay with those who accept the message and to trust God with the people's response. Jesus refers to a custom in which Jews would shake the "unclean" dust of foreign soil from their feet before entering Israel from Gentile territory, a gesture equal to saying "good riddance!" By practicing this custom, the disciples are warning the people who refuse to hear the message of God's kingdom that they are no better than unbelieving Gentiles. Such a strong rebuke might cause some to change their attitudes.

News of the disciples' God-given success spreads to high levels of government. Some say the prophets of old have returned or that John the Baptist has been raised from the dead. Herod has real reason to be terrified if John is alive. Mark 6:14-29 explains that Herod married Herodias, his brother Philip's wife, and imprisoned John for denouncing the marriage. Because Herod recognized John as *"righteous and holy"* (Mark 6:20), he feared harming him. Herod liked to hear John but was puzzled by his preaching. Eventually, due to fulfill a foolish oath, Herod had John executed.

Feeding the Multitude

When the disciples return from their first mission, Jesus takes them to Bethsaida to rest. A crowd interrupts their retreat. Jesus welcomes the people, preaching and healing the sick. Likely resenting the intrusion, the disciples suggest that Jesus send the crowd away to find food. He rejects their request, saying, *"You give them something to eat"* (Luke 9:13).

The disciples have just five loaves of bread and two fish. Their solution—to buy food for everyone—is impossible. Jesus has a different plan. After thanking God, He breaks the bread and fish. Then the disciples distribute the food to the crowd of 5,000 men. Counting women and children, the crowd may have numbered 15,000. The disciples feed the entire multitude, with 12 baskets of leftover food!

Think about how Jesus gave the disciples an impossible task. But He also gave them specific directions. Their job was to obey Him. Will you obey God if He asks you to do the "impossible"? As with the disciples, He will give you what you need to accomplish the task. All He asks is your obedience. He will do the rest.

Jesus' Identity

Alone with His disciples, Jesus asks, *"Who do the crowds say that I am?"* (9:18). They reply that people think He is John the Baptist, Israel's most recent prophet, come back to life. Others think He is Elijah or another prophet, like those who spoke on God's behalf during Israel's past. The crowds don't grasp that God's Son is with them. Although many people have anticipated the Messiah's coming, no one recognizes that Jesus could be their long-awaited deliverer.

Jesus then asks who the disciples think He is. Peter replies, *"The Christ of God"* (9:20). The word *Christ* is the equivalent of the Hebrew title *Messiah (the Anointed One)*. Jesus tells Peter, *"Flesh and blood has not revealed this to you, but my Father who is in heaven"* (Matthew 16:17). One can recognize Jesus' divinity only through the Holy Spirit. Jesus warns His disciples not to tell anyone who He is. To accomplish His purpose on the Cross, He must gradually present Himself as the suffering Savior.

The Cost of Discipleship

Following Jesus requires denying oneself and taking up one's cross. The Jews saw the cross simply as an instrument of punishment, rejection, and death. Rome crucified "enemies of the empire." Here, Jesus explains that true disciples must be willing to endure daily rejection and persecution as they commit their lives to God. He discusses choices and consequences. Those who try to preserve their lives by rejecting Christ and conforming to the world's demands will ultimately lose the life they originally sought. Those who deny themselves to follow Christ will gain eternal life. Although Jesus was required to die a painful and unjust death, He was faithful to His Father's will. Christ's disciples are called to follow His example of obedience.

At the end of the age, those who deny Jesus must pay a price. In the future, Jesus will honor those who honor Him. Those who dishonor Him, He will dishonor. What we sow in this life, we will reap in the life to come.

Luke concludes this passage with Jesus' prediction: *"There are some standing here who will not taste death until they see the kingdom of God"* (9:27). Jesus is likely referring to the Transfiguration, which occurs a week later.

Personalize this lesson.

☑ God calls us to be His servants. We can speak a timely word to a friend in need or encourage another with a spiritual insight. We can take God's healing to a needy world by praying for the sick, visiting the lonely, and showing kindness to those who have suffered injustice. In our own strength, we are inadequate, but by His Spirit, Jesus gives us authority and power. We *"can do all things through Him who strengthens me* [us]*"* (Philippians 4:13). In what ways have you witnessed God strengthening you to accomplish things you know you couldn't do on your own?

Lesson 13

Knowing and Following Jesus
Luke 9:28-62

Memorize God's Word: Luke 9:62.

❖ Luke 9:28-36—The Transfiguration

1. Describe Jesus' appearance during this unusual occurrence. (See also Matthew 17:1-8; Mark 9:2-13.)

2. What does this event reveal about Jesus?

3. Moses and Elijah appear with Jesus. How does their presence provide hope for all believers?

4. What do the disciples hear that proves God's complete satisfaction in Jesus? (See also Matthew 17:5).

❖ Luke 9:37-45—A Father's Request

5. In what three ways does Jesus restore the boy (Luke 9:42)?

_____

_____

6. How do the people respond to this miracle?

_____

_____

_____

7. Why do the disciples misunderstand Jesus' clear, specific statement (9:44)?

_____

_____

8. Why do you think they are afraid to ask Him to explain it to them?

_____

_____

_____

9. What statements has Jesus made that you find hard to understand? Where do you go for explanation?

_____

_____

_____

❖ Luke 9:46-56—True Greatness and Grace

10. Because the disciples do not grasp the nature of God's kingdom or the seriousness of the Lord's mission of suffering and dying for our sin (9:45), they behave as selfish, immature children. What is the difference between *child-like* and *childish*?

_____

_____

11. How does the *"great"* referred to in verse 48 differ from the typical idea of greatness?

_____

_____

_____

12. Why, at this particular time, do you think John says what he does (verse 49)?

_____

_____

13. What does Jesus' answer in verse 50 show about both judgment and tolerance?

_____

_____

14. Considering Jesus' instructions (Luke 9:5), why does He rebuke James and John (verse 55)?

_____

_____

15. How does this incident encourage you?

_____

_____

❖ Luke 9:57-62—Counting the Cost

16. Identify the three requirements of discipleship seen in this passage.

　a.　_____

　　　_____

　b.　_____

　　　_____

　c.　_____

　　　_____

17. What does these requirements communicate to you about the cost of following Jesus?

_____

_____

❖ Luke 9:28-62—Review

18. Read 2 Peter 1:16-18; 1 John 1:1-4.

    a.   What lasting impressions were made on Peter and John from their experience of the Transfiguration?

_____

_____

    b.   How have you experienced Jesus' power and glory?

_____

_____

_____

_____

Apply what you have learned. In knowing and following Jesus Christ we discover purpose, satisfaction, and fulfillment in our lives. Let's seek to know Him more fully and to follow Him sincerely. The first disciples came to know Jesus by living with Him daily, and by hearing His teachings and viewing His miracles. As a believer 2,000 years removed from Jesus' days in a physical body, what elements and tools are available to you to aid you in knowing Him more fully? How can you make better use of these tools this week?

Knowing and Following Jesus
Luke 9:28-62

Jesus Is Glorified

After Peter confesses Jesus is the Christ, the Lord leads him, James, and John up a mountain. While praying, Jesus' face changes and His clothes shine with unearthly brightness. The Transfiguration confirms Peter's confession of faith. Moses and Elijah appear with Jesus. Moses, God's chosen deliverer from Egyptian bondage, foreshadows Christ—God's ultimate deliverer from sin's bondage. Elijah, the great Old Testament prophet, was prophesied to come *"before that great and awesome day of the* LORD*"* (Malachi 4:5). The appearance of an "Elijah" would be a sign to Israel of the Messiah's arrival and the start of a new chapter in the nation's history. The appearance of these two with Jesus symbolically reminds us that Old Testament laws and prophecies are fulfilled in Christ.

As Moses and Elijah discuss Jesus' departure, the disciples become fully aware of Jesus' glory. Peter blurts out his desire to build shelters for the three. A voice from heaven then calls out and confirms Jesus as God's Son. When the disciples hear this, they are terrified and fall to the ground. They look up and see only Jesus. He tells them not to speak of this event until after He *"is raised from the dead"* (Matthew 17: 9).

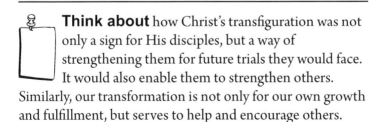

Think about how Christ's transfiguration was not only a sign for His disciples, but a way of strengthening them for future trials they would face. It would also enable them to strengthen others. Similarly, our transformation is not only for our own growth and fulfillment, but serves to help and encourage others.

A Lack of Faith

Jesus and the disciples come down the mountain the next day. A man from the crowd asks Jesus to help his demon-possessed son. Despite the man's begging, the disciples have been unable to drive out the evil spirit. Jesus' response (verse 41) may seem harsh; Matthew's account helps clarify His statement. Matthew says that after Jesus casts out the demon, He tells the disciples, *"If you have faith like a grain of mustard seed … nothing will be impossible for you"* (Matthew 17:20). Perhaps after receiving power and authority to cast out demons, the disciples either waver or, through lack of prayer, forget the true source of their authority—Jesus.

Jesus Foretells His Suffering

Jesus heals the boy, and the crowd marvels at what has happened. Afterward, He tells His disciples He will be betrayed. He, who has power over evil spirits, will be handed over to men. The disciples still do not understand His mission, even after spending three years with Him. They hope for a political Messiah who will free them from Roman rule, but Jesus will save humanity through His suffering.

A Selfish Argument

Soon after Jesus talks to them, the disciples argue over which of them will be greatest. Jesus rebukes them by using a child as an object lesson. Children—innocent, humble, dependent—care most about being loved. The world's value system judges greatness by appearance, achievements, possessions, and power. Strength is revered, while weakness is despised.

Jesus explains that His heavenly Father delights in those with tender, humble hearts who need and depend on God, considering God's desires more important than their own. He explains that welcoming children— ordinary, "unimportant" people—is like welcoming Christ and the Father (Luke 9:48). Jesus wants His followers to demonstrate *childlikeness*: simplicity, love, and honesty. The arguing disciples display the immature qualities of *childishness*: an inability to reason and a lack of wisdom.

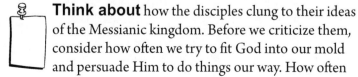

Think about how the disciples clung to their ideas of the Messianic kingdom. Before we criticize them, consider how often we try to fit God into our mold and persuade Him to do things our way. How often might we fail to hear or understand Him when His plan is different from ours?

An Attitude of Intolerance

When John complains of a stranger driving out demons in Jesus' name, Jesus says, *"Do not stop him, for the one who is not against you is for you"* (9:50). This man does what the disciples do—he gathers souls for Jesus. Jesus and the disciples continue their journey to Jerusalem. Some Samaritans refuse to welcome Jesus because He is traveling to Jerusalem through their region. Samaritans and Jews hated each other (John 4:9). John and James, known as *"Sons of Thunder"* (Mark 3:17), ask if they should call down fire from heaven to destroy the Samaritans. Jesus understands the Samaritans' bitterness over the hostile way the Jews have treated them. Jesus rebukes His disciples and leads them to another town. Later, the Samaritans openly received the gospel (Acts 8:4-8).

The Hand to the Plow

Many want to "join the team" but have not counted the cost of discipleship. Jesus is about to go to Jerusalem to be arrested, tortured, and executed. He pays a high price for obeying the Father.

The cost becomes clear in Jesus' encounters with three potential disciples. The first says he will follow Jesus anywhere. Jesus explains that convenience is not guaranteed—a disciple may have to leave family, friends, and home. A second man tells Jesus he must first bury his father (whose death may be years away). Following Jesus must always be the highest priority, even over family. The third man pledges his loyalty to Christ, but wants to tell his family good-bye. Jesus says he must leave the life he has known without looking back.

Discipleship requires discipline and focus. A farmer must look forward, paying attention to the field he is plowing. In the same way, a disciple must be devoted to the One he follows and manage his entrusted responsibility carefully. The Lord wants our complete commitment. Being fit for service in His kingdom requires our willingness to obey the first Commandment: *"Love the LORD your God with all your heart and with all your soul and with all your might"* (Deuteronomy 6:5).

Personalize this lesson.

✓ As we follow Jesus, we, like the disciples who witnessed the Transfiguration, discover that Christ is much more than we currently know. Jesus is revealed to us as Savior when we first believe in Him, and further revealed as our Lord as we walk with Him in obedience. When you asked Him to be the Lord of your life, was it a surprise to find He had taken you at your word and was starting to work His lordship into your life? If you had not counted the cost at first, maybe you discovered the price later. Jesus tells us to stop a particular activity, end a certain relationship, or ask forgiveness of one we hurt. Maybe the price of obedience costs us our pride, the acceptance of others, or the loss of familiar comforts. Yet, as we continue to follow, we discover all has been worth it. Paul wrote, *"I count everything as loss because of the surpassing worth of knowing Christ Jesus my Lord"* (Philippians 3:8). In what ways have you seen this attitude becoming the norm in your life?

Serving and Loving
Luke 10

Memorize God's Word: Luke 10:27.

❖ Luke 10:1-12—Jesus Commissions the Seventy-two

1. Jesus sends 72 disciples to places He plans to visit. Why does Jesus send them two by two? (See Ecclesiastes 4:9-10.)

   _____

   _____

   _____

2. What is the specific call to each of us in Luke 10:2?

   _____

   _____

3. What similarities do you see in this passage and Luke 9:1-6?

   _____

   _____

   _____

❖ Luke 10:13-20—Condemnation of Unbelief

4. How does the message of verse 16 apply to people today?

   _____

   _____

5. What do you think Jesus' response (10:18) to the disciples' report means?

    _____

    _____

6. How would you describe the authority Jesus gives His disciples (verse 19)?

    _____

    _____

    _____

7. What warning and reassurance are found in verse 20?

    _____

    _____

❖ Luke 10:21-24—Jesus Rejoices

8. Concerning Jesus' prayer:

    a. Jesus describes His Father as the Lord of heaven and earth. What does verse 21 reveal about human wisdom?

        _____

        _____

    b. How do we come to know the Father and the Son? (See also John 1:12-13; Romans 10:9-10; Ephesians 2:8-10.)

        _____

        _____

        _____

❖ Luke 10:25-37—The Good Samaritan

9. In verse 25, what is the motive of the man who asks Jesus, "*What shall I do to inherit eternal life?*"

    _____

    _____

10. How would you describe what happens to the traveler and his resulting condition?

_____

_____

_____

11. What is true of all three passersby?

_____

_____

12. Why does Jesus identify the compassionate helper as a Samaritan? (See also Luke 9:52; John 4:9.)

_____

_____

13. As seen from the injured man's perspective, who is his true neighbor?

_____

_____

14. How does Jesus show Himself to be the neighbor of the *"lawyer"* (10:25)?

_____

_____

15. How can you be a true neighbor to someone in your life?

_____

_____

❖ Luke 10:38-42—Jesus Visits Mary and Martha

16. Have you ever felt as Martha did (verse 40)? Describe a similar situation in your life.

_____

_____

_____

17. What does Jesus mean when He says, *"One thing is necessary"* (10:42)?

_____

_____

_____

18. What do you think Mary and Martha may have learned from this encounter?

_____

_____

_____

19. What have you learned from it?

_____

_____

_____

_____

Apply what you have learned. We are called to *"serve the* LORD *with gladness"* (Psalm 100:2).
We need to be careful that our service *for* Christ doesn't keep us from being *with* Christ. Time spent with Him in prayer, worship, and Bible study equips us to love Him more. You are doing this Bible study, so obviously you are spending time with God through His Word. Good for you! Now think about how prayer, worship, or Scripture meditation could help you grow even closer to Him. Pick one area to focus on this week.

Serving and Loving
Luke 10

Laborers Sent Into the Harvest

As the first New Testament missionary, Jesus sent out His 12 disciples to preach and to heal. Now, He sends 72 more witnesses in pairs to the places He plans to visit. The Lord knows that many hungry souls are ready to receive Him. He has trained these disciples well, but they are few compared to all who need to hear the gospel. Thus, He urges His followers to ask the Father to provide more laborers.

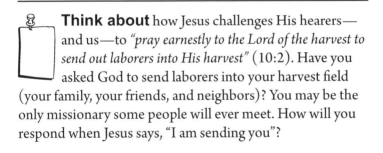

Think about how Jesus challenges His hearers—and us—to *"pray earnestly to the Lord of the harvest to send out laborers into His harvest"* (10:2). Have you asked God to send laborers into your harvest field (your family, your friends, and neighbors)? You may be the only missionary some people will ever meet. How will you respond when Jesus says, "I am sending you"?

The missionaries must take nothing with them, nor delay their mission by visiting people on the way. Towns that reject His message will face terrible consequences, as symbolized by the disciples wiping the dust off their feet. Jesus cries *"woe"* (10:13, 15) to three Galilean towns that have apparently rejected the gospel. In fulfillment of His prophecy, these towns were destroyed during the Roman-Jewish war. We trust that, when judgment fell, God was merciful to the people He called His own in these towns.

The Father has given the Son authority to share the message of salvation.

The Son has given authority to His followers to proclaim the gospel. Jesus' disciples are His authorized representatives. If people reject them, they reject Jesus and, ultimately, God. The close relationship between Jesus and His followers remains true today (2 Corinthians 5:20).

The 72 disciples return from their mission with joy, saying, *"Lord, even the demons are subject to us in Your name!"* (Luke 10:17). Their success comes from the Holy Spirit's power in them. Their true joy should rest not in their victory over evil spirits, but that their *"names are written in heaven"* (10:20), signifying their reconciled relationship with God.

"No one knows who the Son is except the Father, or who the Father is except the Son and anyone to whom the Son chooses to reveal Him" (10:22). Again, we see the connections among the Father, the Son, and the Son's disciples. A person can know God the Father only by first coming to God the Son: *"No one comes to the Father except through Me"* (John 14:6). If by faith we receive Jesus, then we also receive the Father because, as Jesus says, *"Whoever has seen Me has seen the Father"* (14:9).

The Good Samaritan

An expert in the Law tests Jesus by asking what he must do to gain eternal life. Jesus asks him what the Law says. The man answers correctly in saying we are to love God and our neighbor. Jesus tells him to apply these truths to his life. Wanting to justify himself, the man asks Jesus to define *"neighbor"* (Luke 10:29). Jesus answers with a parable that begins on a road from Jerusalem to Jericho. Traveling between the two cities meant descending or ascending 3,000 feet of narrow, winding, rocky road.

On this road, robbers attack a man, leaving him to die. A priest sees him first. Knowing that even touching a dead body would make him ceremonially unclean (Numbers 19:11), the priest crosses the road to avoid the dying man. A Levite, who serves God in the temple, does the same thing. Finally, a Samaritan—a person from a group despised by Jews—comes along. He cleans and bandages the victim's wounds and places him on his own donkey. This means the Samaritan will have to complete his journey on foot. Upon arriving, he pays for the man's room, and even promises to return and reimburse the innkeeper for any extra expenses.

Jesus then asks, *"Which of these three, do you think, proved to be a neighbor to the [victim]?"* (Luke 10:36). The expert in the Law rightly replies, *"The one who showed him mercy"* (10:37). Jesus tells him to do likewise.

 Think about how Jesus says we are to love our neighbors in words and in deeds. Our faith is proven by our actions. Yet, we are not saved because of good works—we do good works because we are saved.

Jesus Visits Mary and Martha

Mary and Martha welcome Jesus and His disciples into their home in Bethany, a village about two miles from Jerusalem (John 12:1-2). Martha, busy preparing food for her guests, is frustrated when Mary sits listening to Jesus instead of helping. When Martha complains to Jesus, He replies, *"You are anxious and troubled about many things, but one thing is necessary. Mary has chosen the good portion, which will not be taken away from her"* (Luke 10:41-42). At the time, women did not join men in listening to a rabbi teach. Jesus changes this practice. It is more important for His followers to hear Him, even if it means missing an elaborate meal.

While imperfect, Martha has good qualities we can learn from. When Jesus comes to raise Lazarus from the dead, He shares with her (not Mary) a powerful statement about eternal life: *"I am the resurrection and the life. Whoever believes in Me, though he die, yet shall he live, and everyone who lives and believes in Me shall never die"* (John 11:25-26). Martha affirms this in one of the clearest statements of faith found in the Bible: *"Yes, Lord; I believe that you are the Christ, the Son of God, who is coming into the world"* (11:27).

In John 12:1-2, we see Martha again showing her love for Jesus through practical acts of hospitality and service. On the other hand, the more spiritually sensitive Mary demonstrates her love for Jesus by anointing His feet with costly ointment. Each woman expresses devotion to Jesus in her own way. Whether you are a "Martha" or a "Mary," there is a place for you in God's kingdom and a task that only you can do.

Personalize this lesson.

✓ Luke 10 gives us a picture of various kinds of service for the Lord. The 72 disciples faithfully spread the gospel message. The Good Samaritan helped a man in need. Martha provided hospitality for the Lord and her guests. In whatever way we serve Jesus, our motivations should bring Him glory, inspire others to know Him, and advance God's kingdom. When we do something to win the approval of others, to be seen as spiritually superior, or to be accepted by a certain group, we are serving for the wrong reason. Most of all, our serving must never be a substitute for deepening our relationship with Jesus and for getting to know the God we serve. Time for prayer, worship, Bible study, and meditation on God's Word should always come before our service. Will you take time right now to sit at Jesus' feet and grow to love Him more, so that your service to Him will be the result of heartfelt gratitude?

Jesus and Prayer
Luke 11:1-36

Memorize God's Word: Luke 11:9.

❖ Luke 11:1-4—Jesus Teaches on Prayer

1. What does 11:1 reveal about Jesus', John the Baptist's, and the disciples' view of prayer?

   _____

   _____

2. What does the word *"Father"* reveal about God's character (11:2)?

   _____

   _____

3. What does it mean to *hallow* God's name?

   _____

   _____

   _____

4. What areas in Jesus' prayer address people's needs?

   _____

   _____

   _____

5. What are the two kinds of forgiveness we can experience?

   _____

   _____

6. In what way might your answers to the previous question make a difference in your prayer life?

❖ Luke 11:5-13—Persistence in Prayer

7. What is the major point of the parable in verses 5-8?

8. What progression do you see in first *asking*, then *seeking*, and finally *knocking*?

9. How do verses 5-10 emphasize boldness and persistence in receiving answers to prayer?

10. By using the example of earthly fathers (11:11-12), what does Jesus try to communicate about His heavenly Father?

11. Why does Jesus speak of the gift of the *"Holy Spirit"* in relation to the *"good gifts"* (11:13) earthly fathers give their children?

12. Read Matthew 7:7-12. Note the differences between the two accounts. What does Luke's version emphasize about Jesus' teaching?

❖ Luke 11:14-20—Jesus Teaches About Prayer and Beelzebub

13. After reading this passage, what is your understanding of Beelzebub?

_____

_____

14. The people react with unbelief and try to discredit Jesus. How does He reply to their accusation?

_____

_____

❖ Luke 11:21-28—Jesus Relates Additional Parables

15. Who do the phrases *"strong man"* and *"one stronger"* (verses 21-22) refer to?

_____

16. What happens to those who are indifferent to Jesus?

_____

_____

17. When an evil spirit leaves a person, why is it dangerous for that void to be left unoccupied?

_____

_____

18. Who lives in every believer? (See 1 Corinthians 6:19; 2 Corinthians 1:21-22.)

_____

19. What do the verbs *"hear"* and *"keep it"* (11:28) tell you about the condition of being blessed?

_____

_____

❖ Luke 11:29-36—Something Greater

20. How is Jesus' presence in His generation greater than Jonah's presence in his generation and Solomon's in his? (See Jonah 1–3; 1 Kings 10:1-7.)

_____

_____

21. Why does Jesus say, *"This generation is an evil generation"* (11:29)?

_____

_____

22. What does it mean for a person's eye to be *"healthy"*?

_____

_____

_____

_____

Apply what you have learned. The disciples asked Jesus to teach them to pray. They understood that they needed something more in their lives. They saw that Jesus' long hours in prayer made a difference in His life. But prayer can be difficult, so consider using the Lord's Prayer as a daily prayer guide. Meditate on each phrase, not only for its application to your prayers, but also to your daily life. And then pray—it will make a difference.

Jesus and Prayer
Luke 11:1-36

An Intimate Prayer

While on earth, Jesus stayed close to His Father through prayer. The disciples, accustomed to Judaism's formal prayers, ask Jesus how to pray. Responding with what is known as "The Lord's Prayer," Jesus calls God *"Father"* (Luke 11:2). Calling God *Father* implies that He regards and loves us as His children—making this title all the more meaningful to the Jewish disciples.

When we call God Lord, we acknowledge His absolute authority over our lives. To call Him Father means we come to Him based on our relationship with Jesus: *"Because you are sons, God has sent the Spirit of his Son into our hearts, crying, 'Abba! Father!' So you are no longer a slave, but a son, and if a son, then an heir through God"* (Galatians 4:6-7). The prayer Jesus gave the disciples—The Lord's Prayer—serves as a model for us today. This prayer has four main parts:

- ❖ **Acknowledgment of God's Majesty** *"Hallowed be Your name, Your kingdom come"* (Luke 11:2). We honor God's name as holy by not using it carelessly or disrespectfully. Our attitudes, words, and deeds also honor Him. The term *kingdom of God* signifies God's presence as a governing power with absolute authority. When we ask for God's kingdom to come, we are asking Him to rule in our lives and to return to establish His righteous kingdom on earth.

- ❖ **Acknowledgment of Our Daily Needs** *"Give us each day our daily bread"* (11:3). God wants us to trust Him to meet our needs, as He did for the Israelites in the desert (Exodus 16:1-21). They needed to learn to trust God for their most basic needs each day. We must do the same.

❖ **Acknowledgment of Our Need for Forgiveness** *"Forgive us our sins, for we ourselves forgive everyone who is indebted to us"* (Luke 11:4a). As we acknowledge ourselves as sinners whom God has forgiven and accepted, we are able to forgive others who sin against us. To forgive is not always easy, but we can do it by the power of the Holy Spirit living within us.

❖ **Acknowledgment of the Reality of Temptation** *"And lead us not into temptation"* (11:4b). During their desert journey, the Israelites faced many trials. Though they had God's presence day and night (Exodus 40:38), they refused to believe His promises of provision and protection—repeatedly rebelling and giving in to temptation. Believers today are assured of the Lord's constant presence (Matthew 28:20). His Spirit lives in us (1 Corinthians 3:16). If we follow God, we will never face temptations we cannot endure (1 Corinthians 10:13). By asking that God *"lead us not into temptation,"* we acknowledge His leading in our lives.

Persistent Prayer

Jesus tells of a man who, at midnight, asks his friend for bread. At first, the friend refuses, but the man's persistence leads to reward. This parable illustrates God's willingness to meet our needs in response to persistent prayer. Jesus adds, *"Ask, and it will be given to you; seek, and you will find; knock, and it will be opened to you"* (Luke 11:9). Asking, seeking, and knocking show an increasing focus and intensity of our prayers. God wants us to communicate with Him and reach out for Him. If a human father tries to do what is best for his children, how much more will our perfect, loving Father do what is good in our lives?

A Blasphemous Accusation

Teachers of the Law and Pharisees accuse Jesus of casting out demons by the power of Beelzebub (Satan) (Matthew 12:24). To equate the work of God's Spirit with Satan's power is blasphemy, showing an inability to tell the difference between good and evil. Those who cannot recognize good from evil do not see sin itself. As a result, they do not ask for forgiveness and remain unforgiven. That is why blasphemy against the Holy Spirit is unforgivable. People who fear having committed this sin have not done so because their fear indicates both a desire for goodness and a recognition of right and wrong.

Jesus responds to the Pharisees' accusation by saying, *"Every kingdom divided against itself is laid waste, and a divided household falls. And if Satan also is divided against himself, how will his kingdom stand?... If I cast out demons by Beelzebul, by whom do your sons cast them out?"* (Luke 11:17-19). Some of the Pharisees' supporters claimed to exorcise demons. So by accusing Jesus, they are saying their own followers do Satan's work as well.

Jesus further states that if His power is from God, then *"the kingdom of God has come upon* [them]*"* (11:20). The King is present in the person of Jesus Christ, and the powers of evil are being overthrown. Neutrality is not an option; the one who does not support Christ opposes Him. Jesus ends His discussion by saying it is not enough to be set free from a demon; one must be filled with the Holy Spirit, too. He uses the illustration of a house that has been cleaned but left empty. A changed life that lacks God's presence is open to reoccupation by even greater evil.

Privilege and Responsibility

A woman in the crowd praises Mary for being especially blessed. Jesus does not deny his mother's unique role, but states that the eternal blessing of belonging to God's kingdom—proven by hearing and obeying God's Word—is a greater privilege than a physical relationship to Him.

Jesus then calls the crowd *"an evil generation. It seeks for a sign, but no sign will be given to it except the sign of Jonah"* (11:29). The Jews knew of Jonah's calling to preach to the Ninevites and about the Queen of Sheba's visit to King Solomon, which Jesus also mentions. Jesus is implying that one greater than Jonah, King Solomon, or any other Old Testament figure stands before them. Despite seeing Jesus' miracles and hearing His teaching, many still doubt. To begin our relationship with God, a step of faith is necessary, but we must take further steps of obedience to grow in our relationship. When we reflect Jesus through our lives and words, people see His light.

Personalize this lesson.

✓ Some people regularly recite "The Lord's Prayer" (Luke 11:2-4). Others use it as a shell or a template upon which to build their prayers. It's a very short prayer that certainly can be prayed verbatim, and it does indeed serve well as a foundation for building longer prayers. But have you ever wondered why the prayer Jesus gave when the disciples asked Him to teach them to pray was so short? Was He just brushing them off? Certainly not. While His "template" prayer was brief, His response continued as He spoke of the persistent petitioner. His sample prayer provides important guidelines for prayer, but Jesus seemed to see persevering faith as being at least as important as providing guidelines. Jesus' story of the persistent petitioner was nearly seven times the length of His sample prayer. Knowing what to pray is good, if we actually pray—and keep praying until God answers. How confident are you that God will answer you when you pray? Is there any prayer request that you have stopped praying because you didn't get an answer the first or second time you "knocked"? Ask God to increase your faith in Him—that He really will answer when you call on Him. Then pick up that prayer request and keep praying it until He answers.

Jesus Challenges Hypocrites
Luke 11:37-12:12

❖ Luke 11:37-44—Jesus Criticizes Pretenders

1. The Pharisees were a religious group who carefully kept the Law of Moses and the unwritten traditions of the Jewish elders. What is the main reason Pharisees wash their hands before eating? (See Mark 7:3-4.)

   _____

   _____

   _____

2. According to Jesus, how does a person become pure and clean?

   _____

   _____

3. Why are the Pharisees' ceremonial hand-washings and tithes ineffective in helping them spiritually?

   _____

   _____

   _____

4. What is wrong with enjoying the best seat in the synagogue and salutations in the marketplace?

   _____

   _____

   _____

5. What are the underlying sins Jesus confronts in the Pharisees?

_____

_____

❖ Luke 11:45-54—Jesus and the Experts in the Law

6. Why is an expert in the Law troubled by Jesus' words to the Pharisees?

_____

_____

7. Why is the honor that the experts in the Law give to the prophets in vain?

_____

_____

8. How does our attitude toward people who speak the truth show our real attitude toward the truth itself?

_____

_____

9. What do verses 53-54 demonstrate about the heart condition of the Pharisees and teachers of the Law?

_____

_____

❖ Luke 12:1-3—Jesus Speaks Against Hypocrisy

10. What does Jesus mean when He compares hypocrisy to leaven or yeast?

_____

_____

11. What does Jesus caution the disciples to be careful of? (See also 1 Corinthians 5:6-8.)

_____

12. We have all been angry or defensive at being rightly rebuked. What does this tell you about your heart condition at the time?

_____

_____

13. a.   How will the *"leaven"* mentioned in 12:1 be exposed?

_____

_____

b.   What guidance does this give you for your life today?

_____

_____

❖ Luke 12:4-7—Jesus Warns and Encourages His Disciples

14. What is the implication of the word *"friends"* (12:4) as Jesus uses it? (See John 15:14-15.)

_____

_____

15. How can we be free from fear of those who can kill the body?

_____

_____

_____

16. What should be our only genuine fear? (See Ecclesiastes 12:13; Isaiah 8:13.)

_____

_____

17. God cares for us personally and knows every detail about each of us (12:6-7). How can you apply this truth to your life today?

_____

_____

_____

❖ Luke 12:8-12—Acknowledging Christ

18. How does verse 10 relate to Luke 11:14-23?

_____

_____

19. a. Read Matthew 12:24-32. What is blasphemy against the Holy Spirit?

_____

_____

    b. Why is this the unforgivable sin?

_____

_____

20. How are we to handle a situation in which we must speak of Christ before people (Luke 12:11)?

_____

_____

21. Jesus predicts persecution for His followers. What is our responsibility to God and to those believers who suffer persecution today? (See Hebrews 13:3.)

_____

_____

Apply what you have learned. The powerful people and institutions in this world are too strong to fight against alone. The Holy Spirit enables us to withstand and triumph over all the power people use to oppose the gospel. Without Christ we are hopeless; with Christ, we are victors. As a Christian, are you a victor only when you feel victorious? What can others see in your life that tells them you are a victor through Christ?

Jesus Challenges Hypocrites
Luke 11:37-12:12

Earlier, Jesus refuted the religious leaders' accusations that He cast out demons by Satan's power (11:15). Jesus warned the people of the danger of unbelief and a desire to see signs (11:29), encouraging them to see God's works with eyes full of faith and light (11:34). After hearing Jesus teach, a Pharisee in the crowd invites Him home for a meal. At this dinner, Jesus pronounces six "woes."

Jesus and the Pharisees

Pharisees were a strict Jewish sect (Acts 26:5). These spiritual leaders placed heavy burdens of guilt and legalism on their people (Luke 13:10-17; Matthew 12:1-14). Focusing on the Law and their interpretations of Scripture, they missed basic truths and overlooked the fulfillment of Messianic prophecies in the person of Jesus (John 5:39). They attacked Jesus for loving tax collectors and sinners (Luke 5:27-32) and showing mercy to the unlovely. Pharisees ignored social outcasts, misfits, and the poor (7:39). Most of the Pharisees distrusted Jesus, though later some converted (Acts 15:5).

Jesus surprises His host by eating without ceremonially washing—a rite imposed by the Pharisees. Jesus responds to His host's unspoken judgment, saying, *"Now you Pharisees cleanse the outside of the cup and of the dish, but inside you are full of greed and wickedness"* (Luke 11:39). Our "heart condition" is more important to God than our religious activity. Jesus says religious behavior—including legally correct offerings—must be accompanied by true love for God.

Jesus also confronts the Pharisees' desire to earn people's praise more than God's. He says, *"Woe to you Pharisees! For you love the best seat in the synagogues and greetings in the marketplaces"* (11:43). Ancient

Middle-Eastern marketplaces served not only as shopping centers, but as gathering places and courts, where strangers, suspects, and heretics could be tried. In this public setting, the Pharisees looked for and received the respect they felt they deserved.

The Pharisees, Jesus says, are *"like unmarked graves, and people walk over them without knowing it"* (11:44). Anyone who touched a corpse or a grave was unclean and an abomination to God (Numbers 19:16). Jesus is saying that the Pharisees are like "walking tombs" that cause others to become defiled. The Pharisees clearly understood His meaning—giving them yet another reason to want to kill Him.

Jesus and the Teachers of the Law

Also present at this meal are scribes—experts in the Pentateuch (the first five books of the Old Testament)—who often interpret the Law at the expense of biblical truth and contradict Jesus' teaching. Called *rabbis*, or *teachers*, many served as jurists in the Sanhedrin (Jewish Senate). Scribes taught the oral (unwritten) Law, and, like the Pharisees, often had heated confrontations with Jesus. Here, a scribe protests Jesus' comments (Luke 11:45). Jesus replies that scribes push people to follow burdensome rules, but do not *"touch the burdens with one of your fingers"* (11:46). He also exposes their hypocrisy: They profess admiration for the Old Testament prophets, yet reject contemporary prophets such as John the Baptist and Jesus, the Christ whom all the prophets proclaimed.

Jesus warns that the scribes' generation will be held responsible for the death of the prophets, referring to Cain's killing of Abel (Genesis 4:8) and Zechariah's murder (2 Chronicles 24:20-21). In the Hebrew Bible, Genesis is the first book and 2 Chronicles is the last. Thus, their entire Bible is a witness against them. Jesus is not saying the scribes are *personally* responsible, but people *just like them* were. Men like these will eventually crucify God's own Son.

Lastly, Jesus charges the scribes with taking *"away the key to knowledge"* (Luke 11:52). The key to understanding Scripture is Jesus Christ. Because the scribes did not accept Him as the Messiah, they could not lead others to Him. In Jesus' day, Scripture was recorded on scrolls kept in the temple and synagogues. Without a personal copy, the people depended on scribes to interpret and clearly explain God's Law. Instead, they heard confusing sermons with impossible demands.

Think about how it is possible to fall into the same sin as the Pharisees—to focus on the outward observance of faith, but not its true meaning. If we do this, we become like them: self-righteous and judgmental, closed to the Holy Spirit's work. The Pharisees responded to Jesus just as their ancestors responded to the prophets—scorning, hating, and even killing them. The scribes honored prophets their own ancestors had killed, but did not pay attention to the prophets' message. Therefore, they failed to recognize their long-awaited Messiah. In order to avoid the errors of these religious leaders, we need to obey the Scriptures we read and study.

Caution Against Hypocrisy

Surrounded by a huge crowd, Jesus warns His disciples against *"the leaven* [sin] *of the Pharisees, which is hypocrisy"* (12:1). In Greek drama, a hypocrite was a masked actor who imitated the speech and conduct of a character—pretending to be something he was not. In the same way, the Pharisees and scribes covered themselves with a false self-righteousness. Jesus says all that is hidden will be made known on Judgment Day. His followers are not to fear those who can only imprison or kill the body, meaning the Pharisees and scribes in the Jewish Senate. Instead, believers should fear (revere) God, who has eternal power over all.

Jesus then makes a statement that has troubled many: *"One who blasphemes against the Holy Spirit will not be forgiven"* (12:10). In light of the coming of the Holy Spirit who will live in believer's hearts, Jesus warns His followers not to oppose and reject God's Spirit as the Pharisees had (Matthew 12:22-32). To do so is to ask for eternal death, because to refuse the Holy Spirit is to refuse the One who can lead a person to repentance, forgiveness, and eternal life.

Finally, Jesus comforts His followers with the great promise that the Holy Spirit will not only accompany them if they are put on trial, but will inspire them as to what to say. His promise is fulfilled repeatedly during the apostolic age, as recorded in Acts.

Personalize this lesson.

☑ Jesus aimed His harshest criticisms not at those who openly disobeyed God's Law—like thieves or prostitutes—but at respectable, law-abiding religious people. And His assessment of their lives was biting. Hypocrisy is serious, and it can lead to self-deception. We begin to believe our own pretenses, lose touch with reality, and no longer hear the words of reproof and correction we need. How can we guard against these pitfalls? The apostle John offered this reassurance: *"If we say that we have no sin, we deceive ourselves, and the truth is not in us. If we confess our sins, He is faithful and just to forgive us our sins and to cleanse us from all unrighteousness"* (1 John 1:8-9). Asking God to forgive our sins, big and small, cleanses our souls and clears away self-righteousness and self-deception. Then we're able to freely face God—and ourselves. Will you spend some time with God and ask Him to reveal any elements of hypocrisy in your life—and if He does, will you ask Him to help you overcome them?

God and Our Priorities
Luke 12:13-59

Memorize God's Word: Luke 12:33-34.

❖ Luke 12:13-21; Exodus 20:17—Parable of the Rich Fool

1. How would you describe the dispute between the two brothers mentioned in this passage?

   _____

   _____

   _____

2. Why does Jesus respond to the dispute with a teaching on *covetousness* (*desiring what someone else has*)?

   _____

   _____

3. What does greed do to a person's value standards (12:15)?

   _____

   _____

4. Other than desiring material possessions, in what areas of life might covetousness occur?

   _____

   _____

   _____

5. How could the man in Jesus' parable have lived more wisely?

    _____

    _____

6. What does Jesus' parable convey about true wealth?

    _____

    _____

❖ Luke 12:22-34—Do Not Worry

7. a. What illustrations from nature does Jesus use to reveal God's relationship with His creation?

        _____

        _____

    b. What does this tell you about God and about ourselves?

        _____

        _____

8. What does Jesus teach about worry?

    _____

    _____

9. Why should a believer's outlook on life be different from an unbeliever's?

    _____

    _____

10. How does God respond to an individual who has the right priorities?

    _____

    _____

11. How does 12:32 illustrate and illuminate 12:31?

    _____

    _____

12. If our hearts are where our treasure is, what can happen to a heart whose treasure is perishable?

_____

_____

❖ Luke 12:35-40—Watchful Servants

13. What will be the result for the servants who show a godly attitude of readiness?

_____

_____

14. What is the attitude of those who are not watchful servants?

_____

❖ Luke 12:41-48—Faithful or Slothful Servants

15. How is the watchful servant rewarded?

_____

_____

16. How would you describe the thoughts and subsequent actions of the unfaithful servant?

_____

_____

17. How would you explain the relationship between

    a.   disobedience done in ignorance and its corresponding punishment?

_____

_____

    b.   greater insight and ability and its corresponding responsibility?

_____

_____

❖ Luke 12:49-59—Division and Interpretation

18. What does Jesus reveal will be one of the results of His mission among people?

_____

_____

19. Would you want a person to become a believer if it is obvious that such a step will produce alienation in that person's family? Please explain your answer.

_____

_____

20. Why is conflict for believers inevitable? (See John 15:18-22.)

_____

_____

21. What were the signs of the times that the people were not interpreting correctly?

_____

_____

22. If the accuser in Luke 12:58 is God, how can we settle matters with Him?

_____

_____

Apply what you have learned. This lesson gives us assurance and warning. Because we are human, we will always be tempted to seek security in God's gifts rather than in God Himself. Trust is not automatic. God has done us the honor of allowing us to choose to trust Him. Have you chosen to trust Him for your eternal salvation? What choices are you making so that you will trust Him to guide your daily life?

God and Our Priorities
Luke 12:13-59

Parable of the Rich Fool

As Jesus teaches the crowd, a man more concerned with money than the truth Jesus is sharing asks Jesus to settle a dispute over his inheritance. Jesus takes the opportunity to warn against greed—a major cause of division, war, and suffering (James 4:1-2). To illustrate, He tells a parable: A farmer, instead of thanking God for his wealth, chooses to *"eat, drink and be merry"* (Luke 12:19), placing his security in wealth rather than in God. God knows his heart and calls him a fool, saying he will die that very night. The man realizes he will lose everything, and be left with nothing of true value to present to God. We often assume we will live a long time, but our lives are brief. We will carry out our plans only if it is God's will (James 4:14-15).

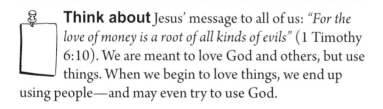

Think about Jesus' message to all of us: *"For the love of money is a root of all kinds of evils"* (1 Timothy 6:10). We are meant to love God and others, but use things. When we begin to love things, we end up using people—and may even try to use God.

Freedom From Anxiety

God has always intended for people to work (Genesis 2:15). When Jesus says not to worry about food and clothing, He is not encouraging laziness; He simply means we must keep our priorities straight. God will surely care for His beloved people. If we have trusted God with our eternal destiny, we can trust Him with our smaller needs. Jesus asks, *"Which of you by being anxious can add a single hour to his span of life?"* (Luke 12:25). Unbelievers worry about their physical needs, but believers can trust that God knows our needs and will supply them. When tempted to worry, we can remember our great value to God and consider His provision.

Instead of pursuing satisfaction from material needs, believers should *"seek His kingdom, and these things will be added to you"* (12:31). Because we trust God to provide for us, we can give generously. As we dispose of distractions, use our talents, and help those in need, we will gain eternal treasure. Jesus gives a warning and a promise: When our treasure is on earth, our hearts will be tied to earthly matters and will decay as things of this world do. But, He promises that if our treasure is in heaven, our hearts will be inclined to do what is godly. Our lives will reflect the nature of our true home (Philippians 3:20).

Prepare to Meet the Master

Jesus' followers must be ready for His sudden return. There are great rewards for *"servants whom the master finds awake when He comes"* (Luke 12:37)—the master will actually serve them. Jesus then describes the faithful servant as a wise manager who is put in charge of distributing good to the other servants. Likewise, God calls us to serve by wisely giving either our money or talents.

Jesus tells us about three disobedient managers. The first is the most openly rebellious and openly defies the master's commands. He will face severe punishment and be assigned a place with *"the unfaithful"* (12:46). The second one knows the master's will but fails to obey and will be penalized, although not as seriously. The third servant does not know the master's instructions, so his disobedience is disciplined less severely.

All are judged according to what they do with their knowledge. *"Everyone to whom much was given, of him much will be required"* (12:48). Knowledge and wealth come with great responsibility. But as children of a fair and faithful God, we are able to obey as we allow the Holy Spirit to influence us.

Three Short Sermons

Jesus continues, *"I came to cast fire on the earth"* (12:49). This is a fire of judgment and purification. Jesus' death on the cross is the climax of this judgment; it is also God's ultimate act of mercy toward us. Jesus died the death we deserve. His coming death on the cross is the *"baptism"* to which He refers (verse 50).

Some expect the Messiah to bring them triumph over enemies and an easy life. Jesus warns that peace with God can cause conflict with others—even division among families. Encountering Jesus and the gospel implies a choice to either receive or reject Christ. When we make choices, lines of separation are drawn—even among people who were once likeminded. We must not be surprised by such opposition.

Jesus explains that people easily interpret signs in nature to predict the weather, but do not understand spiritual signs. They anticipate a storm when clouds appear over the Mediterranean Sea, but do not realize judgment is coming. For centuries, the Jews have had the prophetic Scriptures. They should understand what God is doing presently. They witness Jesus' miracles, yet do not recognize Him as the promised Messiah. Because of persistent unbelief, Israel would miss the most important time of its spiritual history.

Jesus encourages everyone to confess their sin to God and settle accounts with others to avoid the coming judgment. He implies that we are guilty and should acknowledge our guilt before it is too late. If we have committed a crime, we must try to make amends before having to go to court to face a judge's ruling. In the same way, we will all face an eternal Judge. *"If we confess our sins, he is faithful and just to forgive us our sins and to cleanse us from all unrighteousness"* (1 John 1:9). We must act while there is still time (2 Corinthians 6:2).

Personalize this lesson.

✓ As believers, our citizenship is in heaven and the way we live our earthly lives should reflect that fact. It would be foolish to give all our thoughts and energy to things that will pass away. If worries and cares about how to pay the bills, buy clothes for the children, or put food on the table consume you, you can do something. Jesus said, *"Consider ... the lilies"* (Luke 12:27). To *consider* is to *give thought to* and implies a disciplined act. Determine to turn your mind from anxiety and to trust in God's promises. Philippians 4:6-9 says, *"Do not be anxious about anything, but in everything by prayer and supplication with thanksgiving let your requests be made known to God. And the peace of God, which surpasses all understanding, will guard your hearts and your minds in Christ Jesus. Finally, brothers, whatever is true, whatever is honorable, whatever is just, whatever is pure, whatever is lovely, whatever is commendable, if there is any excellence, if there is anything worthy of praise, think about these things. What you have learned and received and heard and seen in me—practice these things, and the God of peace will be with you."* As you intentionally fill you mind with truths like these, you will gradually displace worry and fear and find God's peace taking their place. What Scripture will you choose to begin meditating on today?

Sin and the Kingdom of God
Luke 13

❖ Luke 13:1-9—Produce or Perish

1. What might the people assume about the men who were killed while presenting their sacrifices to God?

   _____

   _____

2. How does Jesus correct His listeners' false understanding of the relationship between sin and suffering?

   _____

   _____

   _____

3. Every day, Christians die, so how do you explain the statement in verse 3, *"Unless you repent, you will all likewise perish"*? (See John 3:16; 11:25-26.)

   _____

   _____

   _____

❖ Luke 13:10-17—Healing on the Sabbath

4. What do you learn about the woman in this passage?

   _____

   _____

5. Why would the synagogue ruler react in anger to the woman's healing?

_____

_____

6. Why is it proper for Jesus to heal the woman on the Sabbath?

_____

7. How have you seen the synagogue ruler's attitude displayed among Christians today?

_____

_____

8. How does Jesus' reply affect your priorities?

_____

_____

❖ Luke 13:18-21—Jesus Describes the Kingdom of God

9. How does verse 18 relate to the episode in the synagogue?

_____

_____

10. How does this parable describe the kingdom of God? (See also Mark 4:30-32.)

_____

_____

❖ Luke 13:22-30; Matthew 7:13-14; John 10:9; 14:6—A Narrow Door

11. a. Jesus is the door. How does He provide access to salvation? (See also John 10:9.)

_____

_____

    b.   Why is the door narrow? (See also Matthew 7:13-14; John 14:6.)

_____

_____

12. How will those outside the door respond once the door is closed?

_____

_____

13. Who will be seen inside this door (13:28)?

_____

14. Where will the others in the kingdom come from?

_____

_____

15. How will positions at the table be decided?

_____

_____

❖ Luke 13:31-35—Jesus' Grief for Jerusalem

16. How does Jesus show courage in the midst of danger?

_____

_____

17. Do you think Jesus is aware of His future suffering? Why, or why not?

_____

_____

18. How do you know that the city of Jerusalem has a special place in Jesus' heart?

_____

_____

19. What does Jesus predict will be the result of the city's unwillingness to embrace Him as Lord?

_____

_____

20. How does He show that He is certain of ultimate victory?

_____

_____

Apply what you have learned. Jesus' listeners who assumed that *"the Galileans whose blood Pilate had mingled with their sacrifices"* and the *"eighteen on whom the tower in Siloam fell"* were *"worse offenders than all the others"* made the same mistake that Job's "comforters" made—assuming that God metes out all His rewards and punishments in this life. That's a natural human assumption, but the fact is, *"unless you repent, you will all likewise perish."* My healthy, wealthy neighbor who has no relationship with Jesus is just as lost as my poor, sickly neighbor who knows not the Savior. What steps will you take to reach out to your lost neighbors—regardless of their health and status?

Sin and the Kingdom of God
Luke 13

The Need for Repentance

Many Jews believed that suffering was a direct result of sin. Some in the crowd tell Jesus about a group of Galileans killed by Pilate while offering their sacrifices. Reminding them of the 18 who died when a tower fell on them, Jesus rejects the idea that the victims were worse sinners than those spared. The righteous suffer; He Himself will suffer greatly. He seeks to make His listeners aware that because of their sin, they, too, deserve misfortune. Twice He warns, *"Unless you repent, you will all likewise perish"* (Luke 13:3, 5). To emphasize this point, Jesus speaks of an unfruitful fig tree. The tree's owner orders the gardener to cut it down, but the gardener begs him to give it more time. Similarly, God has waited centuries for unfruitful Israel—represented by the fig tree—to repent of their disobedience. Jesus' presence among them is their last chance to produce fruit before a time of judgment comes.

God's Grace Versus Man-Made Regulations

As Jesus teaches in a synagogue on the Sabbath, He heals a crippled woman. The angry synagogue ruler declares, *"There are six days in which work ought to be done. Come on those days and be healed, and not on the Sabbath day"* (13:14). Jesus replies, *"You hypocrites! Does not each of you on the Sabbath untie his ox or his donkey ... and ... water it? And ought not this woman ... whom Satan bound for eighteen years, be loosed from this bond on the Sabbath day?"* (13:15-16). Jesus' critics are humiliated. God gave the Sabbath for the Jews' rest and worship, but hypocritical religious leaders would not lift a finger for a hurting person.

The Kingdom of God

Jesus uses two parables to try to help the Jews understand the kingdom. The first compares His kingdom to a mustard seed—*"the smallest of all seeds, but when it has grown ... it ... becomes a tree, so that the birds ... make nests in its branches"* (Matthew 13:32). Like the mustard seed, God's kingdom begins small, but it grows so that many can take refuge in it. The birds represent the nations and peoples of the world. The second parable concerns yeast hidden in flour. The flour represents the world; the yeast represents the unseen, yet active, influence of God's kingdom. A little yeast affects all of the dough.

Later, as Jesus travels through towns and villages on His way to Jerusalem, someone asks if only a few people will be saved. Instead of answering directly, Jesus challenges His listeners to correctly respond to God's call in their lives. Speaking of Himself as the door, He implies that one must be determined to obey the truth of the gospel: *"Strive to enter through the narrow door"* (Luke 13:24). The door is narrow because it is so exclusive; faith in Christ alone enables people to experience redemption and eternal life (Acts 4:12).

Jesus invites the Jews to be saved through faith, knowing outside influences make committing to Him very difficult. The people will have to humble themselves and admit that their religious beliefs are wrong. Those most deeply invested in the current religious system will face scorn from their peers if they choose to follow Jesus. He warns that a time is coming when the door will no longer be open; thus, people must decide now, while He is in their midst.

Those who refuse to enter through the narrow door will remain outside, when it is closed, although they beg for entrance. One day *"the master of the house"* will say to those who would not enter earlier, *"I do not know you or where you come from. Depart from me, all you workers of evil!"* (13:25, 27). Religious observances and careful Law keeping become sin when they are substituted for hearts open to God.

Jesus says, *"People will come from east and west, and from north and south, and recline at table in the kingdom of God. And behold, some are last who will be first, and some are first who will be last"* (13:29-30). Jesus presents three vivid pictures: the variety of people from distant places who will be part of God's kingdom, the feasting and celebration offered to those who come, and the surprising nature of God's evaluation of people and their lives. Some who are considered important in this life will be among the least honored in God's kingdom. God will highly regard humble and unassuming saints, whose faithful lives went unnoticed. We must remember we see only appearances; God sees reality.

Think about how the spiritual reality God sees is not money, talent, or even the gifts of His Spirit, but how we use these things. The faithful stewardship of a very unassuming gift—helping, for instance—may be more worthy of honor in God's eyes than a great talent not wholly used for Him.

Courage and Compassion

Some Pharisees warn Jesus to leave because Herod wants to kill Him. Though seemingly concerned for His welfare, they probably have ulterior motives for wanting Him to leave their region. Jesus is not moved by fear of Herod. His reply reveals His character and courage: *"Go and tell that fox, 'Behold, I cast out demons and perform cures … and … finish My course'"* (Luke 13:32). From eternity, God planned for His Son to be crucified in Jerusalem at Passover. Jesus is determined to fulfill His purpose for coming into the world.

God had given the Israelites many opportunities to turn to their Messiah, but most had refused. In anguish Jesus cries out, *"O Jerusalem, Jerusalem. … How often would I have gathered your children together as a hen gathers her brood under her wings, and you were not willing!"* (13:34). The tender image of a hen gathering her chicks in the face of danger is familiar to these agricultural people. Jesus longs to protect and save the people of Israel, but most have turned away. They would eventually face the devastating destruction of Jerusalem by the Romans in AD 70—just as Jesus predicted.

Personalize this lesson.

✓ Do you see the flow of chapter 13? Luke begins with Jesus correcting His listeners' mistaken assumption that those who died under Herod's cruelties as well as those who died in the fall of the tower had been divinely punished for especially bad sins. The chapter closes with Jesus mourning the impending disasters coming to Jerusalem for its inhabitants' rejection of Him. Between those two accounts, we see several teachings about the kingdom—as well as an account of a healing, which provides further kingdom insight. Jesus desperately wants everyone to enter His kingdom, but each person must choose to enter. The people of Jerusalem *"were not willing"* to enter on Jesus' terms. Do you at times resist Jesus' terms for kingdom entry (not for eternal salvation, but for daily communion)? What can you do to become more pliable, more *willing*?

Consider the Cost
Luke 14

Memorize God's Word: Luke 14:33.

❖ Luke 14:1-6—Jesus Visits a Pharisee

1. What clues in this passage show the Pharisees' real attitude toward Jesus?

   _____

   _____

   _____

2. a. Based on Exodus 20:8-11 and Isaiah 58:13-14, how would you explain the purposes of the Sabbath?

   _____

   _____

   b. Do you think these purposes apply today? Why or why not?

   _____

   _____

❖ Luke 14:7-14—The Parable of the Wedding Feast

3. How does Jesus' advice about taking the lowest place relate to our spiritual behavior? (See Romans 12:3; James 4:6, 10.)

   _____

   _____

   _____

4. What is the relationship between Luke 14:11 and 13:30?

_____

_____

5. What causes people to use their hospitality for selfish or wrong motives?

_____

_____

6. In light of Luke 14:7-14, what changes might you make in how you show hospitality?

_____

_____

❖ Luke 14:15-24—The Great Banquet

7. The Jews are the invited guests (John 1:11-13). What is your understanding of the banquet invitation?

_____

_____

8. What is meant by the phrase, *"Go out ... and compel people to come in"* (14:23)?

_____

_____

_____

9. As you consider this parable, how does it

    a. encourage you?_____

    _____

    b. challenge you?_____

    _____

    c. warn you? _____

    _____

❖ Luke 14:25-33—The Cost of Discipleship

10. What does verse 26 mean?

_____

_____

11. What is the *"cross"* true disciples are to bear? (See also
    Luke 9:23-24.)

_____

_____

12. What do the illustrations of building a tower and of a king going
    to war tell you about the nature of a genuine commitment to
    Christ?

_____

_____

13. Why is it important to consider the cost of being a true disciple?

_____

_____

❖ Luke 14:34-35—The Flavor of Salt

14. a. Christians are the salt of the earth (Matthew 5:13). What
        are some ways salt can be used?

_____

_____

_____

  b. How are these uses similar to Christians' tasks in the world?

_____

_____

15. a. What are some ways Christians can "lose their saltiness"?

_____

_____

b.   How can we prevent this from happening?

_____

_____

_____

16. Choose a verse or parable from this lesson and explain how it is important to you.

_____

_____

_____

_____

_____

Apply what you have learned. Why, in His parable of the great banquet, did Jesus give such a wide open invitation and then, in His call to discipleship, so dramatically narrow the call? Was it a bait and switch? No. The kingdom is open to anyone. But He wants those who are considering entry to know what they're entering. Entry is simple, and the payoff is tremendous, but those who enter will be persecuted. Have you begun to pay the price for following Jesus? What lessons have you learned about the price for following Jesus?

Consider the Cost
Luke 14

Compassion Over Tradition

One Sabbath, as Jesus dines at a Pharisee's home, other Pharisees are *"watching Him carefully"* (Luke 14:1). Luke uses the Greek *paratereo*, meaning *to observe with sinister intent*. It could be that the Pharisees invited a crippled man to the dinner just to test Jesus. When Jesus asks, *"Is it lawful to heal on the Sabbath, or not?"* (14:3), the Pharisees keep silent. Exodus 20:8-11 forbids labor on the Sabbath. But religious leaders later added complex rules about what counts as labor. After healing the man, Jesus asks the Pharisees another question: Would they pull a son or an ox out of a well on the Sabbath? The Pharisees are silenced again. If they answer this question truthfully, they will expose their hypocrisy.

Humility and Hospitality

As Jesus watches some guests go for the best seats, He warns that seeking honor can lead to humiliation. Jesus knows each person's motives, including the host's, who may have invited important guests hoping they would return his hospitality. Jesus advises him to give a party for those unable to repay his kindness. Such generosity will lead to blessing here on earth and reward at the resurrection of the just.

Jesus challenges His listeners to a new way of thinking, which will change their priorities and worldview. God's kingdom operates on principles radically different from this world's system. According to God's way, *"everyone who exalts himself will be humbled, and he who humbles himself will be exalted"* (Luke 14:11). If we follow this principle, one day we will hear Him say, *"Friend, move up higher"* (Luke 14:10).

Think about the true meaning of hospitality. In Jesus' time, hospitality was offered to strangers weary from traveling. The Pharisees corrupted hospitality by using it to display their wealth and gain favor with "powerful" guests—guests who often tried to sit in the best seats. To be hospitable without any thought of gain is to live in the manner of the heavenly Father (Luke 14:13-14; 1 Peter 4:9). All true hospitality comes from God, the giver of all we have—life, salvation, and the hope of heaven (James 1:17).

Refusal to Enter the Kingdom

A guest mentions the future Messianic banquet, perhaps assuming only Israelites will attend. Jesus responds with a parable that clearly portrays God's invitation of salvation and righteousness as available to all. An invitation to a feast was customarily followed by a summons, making the person well aware of the host's expectations. It would be insulting if a guest who had accepted the invitation now made excuses not to attend. In Jesus' parable, some of the guests do exactly that.

The first man says he must go see his new property. In the context of this parable, putting business first is equivalent to placing it above one's spiritual welfare. The second man says he has to try out a new pair of oxen. Too often, we see caring for our possessions as more important than spiritual concerns. The third guest offers the most reasonable excuse, saying he is recently married. Jewish husbands were to spend the first year at home with their brides (Deuteronomy 24:5). God expects us to lovingly care for our families, but we are not to put them before Him or use them as a reason to deny Him His rightful place in our lives.

When the servant reports the guests' refusal to attend, the master orders him to invite people previously excluded. The servant does, but there is still room. He is sent even farther, to find more guests. In this parable, the original invited guests represent Israel as a nation. Although the Messiah has come, they reject His salvation message (John 1:11). God desires to fill His empty table with those willing to accept His offer. The host then offers banquet invitations (the gospel) to Gentiles.

The Call to Consecrated Discipleship

Earlier, Luke recorded Jesus' remarks to His disciples about the cost of following Him (Luke 9:23-27). Now, Jesus tells the crowds of His requirements for discipleship. Jesus' requirement of coming before any other loyalty may sound hard, but it is the first step toward getting our relationships in proper perspective.

Jesus then discusses the necessity of bearing one's cross. He is not referring to ordinary problems, but to conflicts and trials that result from commitment to Christ. At that time, such commitment often led to facing hostility and persecution from religious authorities. John 9:13-34 records an account of Jesus healing a man born blind. The Jews then cast the man out of the synagogue. Excommunication would affect not only his spiritual life, but his business and social life as well. Later, as members of the early church sought to spread the gospel, many were imprisoned or even killed (Acts 4:1-4; 12:1-3).

Finally, Jesus uses the examples of a man building a tower and a king going to war to show that mere enthusiasm is insufficient. At this point, countless people have heard reports of Jesus' miraculous healings, and they understand that He teaches with greater authority than the Pharisees. Now He encourages people to grow beyond their initial experiences of God's power in order to mature spiritually through the demands of discipleship. Salvation is a free gift, but there is a price to pay for following Christ. Although the price is nothing compared to the blessings God pours on faithful believers, it is more than some are willing to pay.

Those traveling with Jesus that day saw only the blessings of following Him. Even today, some think of Jesus as a magician who "fixes" life's many problems. We must be willing to *"hear"* and accept the difficult challenge of discipleship (Luke 14:35). Jesus' teaching presents a balance: great blessing is experienced in an ongoing relationship with Him, but self-discipline and sacrificial service are also needed. Like the *"salt,"* Jesus calls believers to be different from the unbelieving world. Just as salt preserves and enhances, believers must preserve and enhance the good within our communities. Are we willing to *"hear"* and accept the challenge of discipleship in order to be effective in our faith? If so, we will maintain our saltiness.

Personalize this lesson.

☑ How appropriate that Jesus followed His great banquet parable with a reference to salt, the primary food preservative and seasoning of that era. A salt-free banquet would have been impossible. Disciplined, distinctive Christians are as necessary for the kingdom as salt is for a dinner banquet. Imagine entering a grand banquet hall and sitting down to a meal that looks magnificent but is either spoiled or tastes woefully bland. No matter how good the food looks, if it tastes bad, you probably won't stay—nor will you recommend the banquet to anyone else. Jesus wants everyone, people from all walks of life—*"the poor, the crippled, the lame, the blind"*—to come to His banquet, but if those who enter find the spiritual food (seen in our lives) to be spoiled or bland, the banquet will be a flop. What lessons about God's great love for the lost and man's need for humility did you learn in this lesson that can enhance your "flavor"?

God's Love in Parables
Luke 15

❖ **Luke 15:1-10—The Lost Sheep and the Lost Coin**

   1.   What picture does verse 1 give you?

   2.   What does the Pharisees' reaction tell you about them?

   3.   What encouragement or warning do you find in verses 1 and 2?

   4.   What similarities between the parables of the lost sheep and the lost coin do you notice? What do these themes indicate about God's love for us?

❖ Luke 15:11-19—The Son Who Was Lost

5. How does the loss of the younger son differ from the loss of the sheep and the coin?

    _____

    _____

6. How would you describe the younger son?

    _____

    _____

7. The father surely knows his son's character and lifestyle. Why would he honor his son's request to be given his inheritance immediately?

    _____

    _____

    _____

8. Why does God allow us this same kind of freedom?

    _____

    _____

    _____

9. How does Jesus describe the younger son's realization and eventual change of heart?

    _____

    _____

10. Would this parable be encouraging or discouraging to the parent of a young person who is determined to live life his or her own way? Why?

    _____

    _____

    _____

    _____

❖ Luke 15:20-24—The Father's Reaction

11. What does verse 20 reveal about the father?

_____

_____

12. What does the father's response to his son reveal about God's attitude toward you?

_____

_____

❖ Luke 15:25-31—The Older Son

13. What picture do you get of the older brother's relationship with his father?

_____

_____

14. How would you evaluate the older brother's reaction to his younger brother?

_____

_____

15. With which brother is it easier for you to identify? Why?

_____

_____

16. What do you learn about the father's character from Luke 15:31?

_____

_____

17. What does this parable show you about your attitude toward those who wrong you?

_____

_____

_____

❖ Luke 15:32; Ephesians 2:1-10—Lost and Found

18. How does Luke 15:32 illustrate Ephesians 2:7 and 2:10?

_____

_____

19. How were we (who believe in Christ) once as dead or lost as the younger son?

_____

_____

20. How did we show that we were lost or dead?

_____

_____

21. How would you explain the process through which a person is *"found"* and becomes *"alive"*?

_____

_____

22. How does this person show that he or she is found and alive?

_____

_____

Apply what you have learned. Two facts about God the Father stand out in this chapter: His willingness to go to any lengths to rescue the lost (Romans 5:8) and His loving welcome to all who return to Him. Where do you find yourself in this chapter? Are you waiting for a prodigal to come home? Are you struggling to accept God's compassion toward someone who doesn't seem to deserve it? Talk to God about what this chapter has stirred for you and respond to His loving kindness.

God's Love in Parables
Luke 15

Welcoming Sinners

Jesus calls sinners to repent, but the Pharisees and teachers of the Law do not think sinners can be redeemed. Because of their self-righteousness, they wrongly sense God's approval. As tax collectors and "sinners" gather around Jesus, the religious leaders grumble, *"This man receives sinners and eats with them"* (15:2). Jesus responds by telling three parables about God's love for the lost.

The Lost Sheep

A shepherd leaves his 99 sheep to search for the one that is lost. Dependent and not very smart, sheep could easily lose their way in Israel's rugged country. Unless found quickly, the sheep would die of exposure or be killed by predators. When the shepherd finds his lost sheep, his friends and neighbors rejoice with him.

The Lost Coin

A woman with 10 silver coins (each worth about a day's wages) loses one. She searches carefully for the coin—either because she needs the money or because it is part of a headdress made of 10 silver coins she received as a Jewish bride. Like our wedding rings, the coin symbolizes the marriage covenant and has more than monetary value. Finding the coin, she calls others to celebrate with her. In the same way, *"There is joy before the angels of God over one sinner who repents"* (Luke 15:10). The concept of a loving heavenly Father seeking after lost children was foreign to the Pharisees. They viewed God only as someone who might occasionally forgive a sinner who groveled enough before Him.

The Prodigal Son

The lost sheep strays through ignorance. The coin is lost through no fault of its own. In this parable, a son *chooses* a path of sin. A father has two beloved sons. The younger one asks for his inheritance early—basically wishing his father dead. The father grants his wish.

The son takes his inheritance and leaves home, clearly not intending to return. In the far country, he wastes all his money on sinful living. When famine strikes, he is reduced to feeding pigs (probably owned by a Gentile, as Jews considered pigs unclean animals). He is starving, but cannot even eat their scraps. The pigs are given more consideration and care than he is.

This rebellious son mistakenly thinks he can gain his freedom by doing as he pleases. But Satan is the master deceiver. Rather than gain freedom, the son becomes a slave to sin. When he realizes that his sin has ruined him, he decides to return home. Like the prodigal son, we come to our senses when we admit that we are wrong, we have sinned against God and others, and need God's help to change.

The son heads home, not expecting his father's forgiveness because he knows he is unworthy. He is willing to be taken back as a servant. Because he has been waiting and watching for his son's return, the father sees him approaching from a distance. He does not wait for his son to reach him, but runs to welcome him with hugs and kisses.

Think about what a picture this is of God's love for us! He is ever on the lookout for the returning penitent, ready to enfold him with His love. He forgives and restores. The father in this parable tells his servants to give his son the best clothes (a symbol of family honor), a ring (a symbol of family authority), and shoes (a symbol of family membership). God does that with us when we repent of our sin and He receives us as *"members of* [His] *household"* (Ephesians 2:19).

In the field, the older son hears the celebration over his brother's return. He angrily refuses to join the party despite his father's pleas. The son says, *"These many years I have served you, and I never disobeyed your command, yet you never gave me a young goat, that I might celebrate with my friends"* (Luke 15:29). Although he doesn't see it, the older brother is as lost as his younger brother had been. He has enjoyed his loving father's shelter and provision. Yet he regards his life as nothing better than mandatory servitude. In his bitterness, he calls his brother *"this son of yours"* (15:30), speaking as if there was no relationship between them. He assumes the worst of his younger brother—that he has spent his money on prostitutes. Those who fail to rejoice in their own forgiveness often refuse to forgive others. The older brother's self-righteousness and hard-heartedness resembles the Pharisees' attitudes.

 Think about how some Christians live in spiritual poverty—although they have a loving Father who blesses them greatly. Perhaps the older son never asked for a goat to celebrate with his friends. Sometimes we do not have because we do not ask God (James 4:2). Thus, we live as if we are spiritually poor while all Heaven's resources are available to us. Ask your heavenly Father for His blessing and see how He answers you.

The father—equally loving to both sons—reminds the older son, *"All that is mine is yours"* (Luke 15:31). In Jewish tradition, the oldest son received an inheritance twice as large as that of his siblings. His brother, having already received his inheritance, was entitled to nothing more. The older son would inherit everything else his father owned. The father concludes, *"This your brother was dead, and is alive; he was lost, and is found"* (15:32). Because of their broken relationship, it was as though the son was dead to the father. Similarly, we were once spiritually dead in our sins when separated from God. As the son is now alive again through reconciliation to his father, we who believe are alive in Christ. *"Because of the great love with which He loved us ... even when we were dead in our trespasses, [God] made us alive together with Christ"* (Ephesians 2:4-5). *"God ... through Christ reconciled us to Himself"* (2 Corinthians 5:18).

Personalize this lesson.

☑ Once we were *"separated from Christ ... having no hope and without God in the world. But now in Christ Jesus* [we] *... have been brought near by the blood of Christ"* (Ephesians 2:12-13). We, who once lived far from God, have come to our senses and returned to our heavenly Father. God loves those who are lost and longs for their return. He created us and redeems all who respond to His invitation for salvation. Jesus talked about the return of the sheep, the coin, and the son—all lost from their rightful owner. Similarly, God created each of us, so we rightfully belong to Him. We are His property, redeemed at the cost of His own Son's blood. As we recognize God's unconditional love, our love for Him will surely grow. We will want Him to touch others as He has touched us. If you struggle with jealousy and judgmentalism, will you ask God to help you understand instead of judge, praise rather than criticize, forgive, not condemn? As others come into His kingdom, will you rejoice knowing Jesus is finding the lost and bringing the dead to life? What can you do to make such attitudes a natural part of your life?

Lesson 21

Wisdom and Riches
Luke 16

Memorize God's Word: Luke 16:13.

❖ Luke 16:1-9—The Shrewd Manager

1. How is this steward irresponsible in managing the owner's estate?

   _____

   _____

2. How does the dishonest steward protect his future well-being?

   _____

   _____

3. How can we ensure our future spiritual well-being?

   _____

   _____

4. Why would the master praise the steward for his shrewdness?

   _____

   _____

5. Why do you think many people find this parable difficult to understand?

   _____

   _____

   _____

❖ Luke 16:10-13—A Trustworthy Servant

6. In verse 11, what are *"true riches"*? (See also Luke 12:32-34; James 2:5.)

_____

_____

7. Why is it important that we only serve one master?

_____

_____

_____

❖ Luke 16:14-18—The Hypocritical Pharisees

8. What do we learn about the Pharisees' priorities?

_____

_____

9. How can believers avoid judging others by the Pharisees' standards? (See also 1 Samuel 16:7.)

_____

_____

10. This verse has different interpretations. What do you think Jesus means when He says, *"The kingdom of God is preached, and everyone forces his way into it"* (Luke 16:16)?

_____

_____

_____

11. What hyperbole (exaggeration for effect) does Jesus use to show that the *principles* of the Law—as they relate to a person—still apply?

_____

_____

_____

❖ Luke 16:19-25—The Rich Man and Lazarus

12. How wealthy is the rich man, and what is his relationship to Lazarus?

_____

_____

13. What is each man's eternal future?

_____

_____

14. a. How does the rich man's attitude toward his wealth determine his destination?

_____

_____

 b. In what way does his request to Abraham reveal his character?

_____

_____

❖ Luke 16:26-31—A Great Chasm

15. What does the *"great chasm"* (16:26) tell us about this man's decisions and actions? (See also 2 Corinthians 6:2; Hebrews 9:27.)

_____

_____

_____

16. Considering Luke 16:26, what decisions might you make in order to change your eternal destiny or that of someone else?

_____

_____

_____

_____

17. From his next request, what changes do you note in the rich
    man's attitude?

    _____

    _____

    _____

    _____

Apply what you have learned. Money and
wealth are morally neutral, but our attitude about
them indicates our true values. All we have is a gift
from God, and we must answer to Him as His stewards.
Because Jesus had much to say about wealth and its uses,
we need to use what we have responsibly. *"Do not lay up
for yourselves treasures on earth, where moth and rust destroy
and where thieves break in and steal, but lay up for yourselves
treasures in heaven, where neither moth nor rust destroys and
where thieves do not break in and steal. For where your treasure
is, there your heart will be also"* (Matthew 6:19-21). What
treasures are you storing in heaven?

Wisdom and Riches
Luke 16

The Shrewd Manager

In Jesus' parable of the shrewd manager, a man soon to be fired for wasting his master's money has his own "retirement plan." He tells his employer's debtors to write a reduced amount on the bills they owe, thus obligating the debtors to himself. He has failed his master, because a steward's first duty is to be faithful (1 Corinthians 4:1-2) and then to look for ways to benefit his master. Believers are stewards of what God has given us and are to *"gain friends"* (by helping those in need), who will, in turn, one day welcome us (their benefactors) into heaven. Luke 16:9 is the key to this parable; verses 10-12 are its heart. This steward was unfaithful in a small way, perhaps through carelessness or petty thievery. When his future is in jeopardy, his dishonest nature bursts into full bloom, and he is unfaithful in a much greater sense.

In 16:11-12, Jesus implies that God's people sometimes handle money incorrectly. If we are not faithful with earthly riches, why should we be entrusted with eternal riches? The shrewd steward used money to ensure his earthly future; we are to use money in a way that reflects our spiritual future (Luke 12:33-34). Jesus is not saying money is inherently unrighteous; if so, it would have been unacceptable as an offering to God. We make money unrighteous by misusing it.

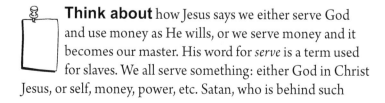

Think about how Jesus says we either serve God and use money as He wills, or we serve money and it becomes our master. His word for *serve* is a term used for slaves. We all serve something: either God in Christ Jesus, or self, money, power, etc. Satan, who is behind such masters, pays his servants with the wages of death, *"but the free gift of God is eternal life in Christ Jesus our Lord"* (Romans 6:23). Are we faithful stewards of all God has given us? Do we share the gospel, using our spiritual gifts to serve Him and others?

The Hypocritical Pharisees

Jesus confronts some scoffing Pharisees about their hypocritical attitudes. They wrongly considered prosperity as God's reward for goodness, tremendously enjoyed parading their "goodness" before men, and thus became an abomination to God. Jesus then says that the Law and the Prophets (the Old Testament) were preached until John the Baptist appeared. John's ministry marks a transition to a new era, and *"the good news of the kingdom of God is preached"* (Luke 16:16). The rest of verse 16 may refer to the passionate response of some to the good news, or that one should receive the gospel with the same kind of zeal that marked those who sought to establish God's kingdom in Israel through physical violence. Because the Pharisees' innumerable rules obscured the original precepts of God's laws and heavily burdened the Jews, Jesus refuted the need to follow them. Instead, by perfectly enforcing and fulfilling the Law, He shows that the Law's nature is eternal and enduring. Thus, Jesus says, *"It is easier for heaven and earth to pass away than for one dot of the Law to become void"* (16:17).

Jesus restates the biblical principle of marriage as an example of the binding character of God's true Law. When asked why Mosaic Law permitted divorce, Jesus said it was because of hard-heartedness (Matthew 19:3-9). The original creation order (Genesis 2:24) regarding marriage was not so; divorce was a concession to humanity's sinful nature. The Bible says it is wrong to break the marriage bond, and remarriage to another is adultery. One error is to think divorce and remarriage is unforgivable. Jesus died so we could be forgiven for our sins. If His death made forgiveness possible and God's love and mercy makes it available for the asking, Christians must be as willing to forgive as God is.

The other error is assuming that because divorce and remarriage can be forgiven, like any other sin, it is not serious. In a failed marriage, both partners suffer, and the children are the most serious casualties. God offers forgiveness and a new start (1 John 1:9). For those struggling with a difficult marriage, the word of comfort is that we are not alone in our trouble.

The Rich Man and Lazarus

The parable in Luke 16:19-31 gives a glimpse of life after death and challenges us to help those in need. The rich man lived luxuriously. Crippled Lazarus lay at the rich man's gate, longing to eat his table scraps. When Lazarus died, he was *"carried by the angels to Abraham's side"*; when the rich man died, he *"was buried"* (Luke 16:22). Lazarus, despite his suffering, clung to God. The rich man catered to his material desires; at his death, his body was buried. The rich man's poor, starved spirit, for which he made no provision in his lifetime, is now tormented in hell (Hades), not because he was rich, but because he had been self-centered, ignoring God and his fellow man.

The rich man, seeing Lazarus far above with Abraham, begs that Lazarus be sent to relieve his agony. He obviously still regards Lazarus as a mere servant. Abraham's reply implies that the rich man had chosen not to be involved with the things of God or others' needs. Now he pays the penalty for his choices. The rich man then asks that Lazarus be sent to warn his five brothers. Abraham says they have the Old Testament to guide them. If that doesn't move them, neither will the witness of one raised from the dead. The rich man, apparently a Jew, should have been familiar with the Old Testament, in which the Law exhorts God's people to help the poor (Leviticus 19:9-10), the prophet Isaiah says to show compassion to the needy (Isaiah 58:7), and Proverbs 29:7; 21:13 say the righteous are those who care for the poor, while the wicked disregard them to their own peril.

Personalize this lesson.

☑ This chapter deals with money and its relationship to eternity. What we do with money reveals what is in our hearts. Consider the way you handle money. What does it say about you? It is not how much money you have, but how you use it that is important. Regardless of how God has chosen to bless us, we all must carefully determine the proper use of what He has given us. Few of us are as poor as Lazarus or as wealthy as the rich man, yet God holds us all responsible for good stewardship of what He has provided. As you remember the parable of the rich man and Lazarus, will you also remember Jesus' words from Luke 6:38? *"Give, and it will be given to you. Good measure, pressed down, shaken together, running over, will be put into your lap."*

The Kingdom of God
Luke 17

❖ **Luke 17:1-10—The Necessity of Faith**

1. What does Jesus say about temptation and the one who causes it?

    _____

    _____

    _____

2. What is a believer's first responsibility toward one who has succumbed to temptation? What responsibility does the offender have?

    _____

    _____

    _____

3. Why are we to forgive the repentant sinner *"seven times in the day"* (17:4)?

    _____

    _____

    _____

4. Why do the disciples ask Jesus to increase their faith at this particular time?

    _____

    _____

    _____

5. How would you paraphrase verse 6 in today's language?

    _____

    _____

    _____

6. What attitude does Jesus warn His disciples about?

    _____

❖ Luke 17:11-19—Gratitude for Healing

7. a. Why do the men with leprosy stand at a distance? (See
        Leviticus 13:45-46.)

        _____

        _____

    b. Why are they to show themselves to the priests? (See
        Leviticus 14:1-3.)

        _____

        _____

8. Explain how faith played a role in their healing.

    _____

    _____

    _____

9. Only one man thanks Jesus for his healing. What does this say
    about the condition of many human hearts?

    _____

    _____

10. According to Psalm 107:19-22. How should we respond when
    God answers a prayer?

    _____

    _____

    _____

11. Why does the man's thankful response seem extraordinary? (See John 4:9.)

_____

_____

❖ Luke 17:20-21—The Kingdom of God

12. As it relates to the kingdom of God, *kingdom* is the realm or domain in which God is preeminent, and in which His will is fulfilled. What does Jesus mean when He says, *"the kingdom of God is in the midst of you"* (17:21)?

_____

_____

13. What has to happen before we can enter the kingdom of God? (See John 3:3, 5-8.)

_____

_____

14. What are we to do to enter the kingdom of God and what are some blessings for kingdom residents? (See Acts 2:38; Romans 10:9-10; 8:16-17; 14:17.)

_____

_____

❖ Luke 17:22-30—The Days of the Son of Man

15. How should we react if someone says that Christ has already returned? (See also Luke 21:8.)

_____

_____

16. Why, in Luke 17:25, in the middle of a discussion on His second coming, would Jesus refer to His death on the cross?

_____

_____

17. How will the time of Jesus' return parallel Noah's time? (See also Genesis 6:5, 11-12; 2 Timothy 3:1-5.)

_____

_____

❖ Luke 17:31-37—One Taken, One Left

18. According to Luke 17:31-33, what value is placed on earthly things?

_____

_____

19. In this context, why is it important to remember Lot's wife? (See Genesis 19:15-26.)

_____

_____

20. Will physical nearness to a believer be a guarantee for safety? Why, or why not?

_____

_____

21. Why does Jesus illustrate His point with a nighttime event and a daytime event?

_____

_____

Apply what you have learned. The best way to be ready for Jesus' return is to be ready to face Him at any time. Do you need to address an area of your life in order to be sure you are ready for His return? Why not address that area now? Don't worry about whether you will be faithful to Him at a time of great testing. You only have to be faithful today. He will give you grace for each succeeding day.

The Kingdom of God
Luke 17

Christians in the World

In chapter 17, Jesus focuses on some key elements of the Christian life—forgiveness, faithfulness, gratitude, and ongoing preparation for the coming *"days of the Son of Man"* (Luke 17:22). Jesus implies that in this world, temptation is inevitable. Although being tempted is not a sin, yielding to temptation *is* sin, because God always gives us a way of escape (1 Corinthians 10:13). Jesus was tempted, yet He was without sin (Hebrews 4:15). In Luke 17:1, the word translated *"sin"* (Greek, *scandalon*) means *scandal, offense,* or *stumbling block.* *"Little ones"* (Luke 17:2) are those who are young, either in faith or in years. Consequently, Jesus warns His disciples to *"pay attention to yourselves!"*

If a fellow Christian sins, Jesus' followers are to rebuke the offender, but forgive if he or she repents. God wants us to forgive, just as He offers us divine forgiveness because Christ paid the penalty for our sins. No sin is beyond the scope of His redeeming love. Realizing they cannot forgive on their own, the disciples ask Jesus to increase their faith. His reply concerns the smallest seed sown in that region, which grows huge due to the essential element of life within it; the seed's size is not important. So it is with faith. The object of faith is more important than the size of one's faith. The disciples are not to take pride in what their faith enables them to do. Jesus says a servant is responsible for doing his best; he is not constantly thanked for doing his duty. Likewise, God's servants are to be faithful, not expecting praise for obedience.

The Sin of Ingratitude

Traveling to Jerusalem, Jesus sees 10 lepers, one a Samaritan. By Law, lepers had to *"live alone ... outside the camp"* (Leviticus 13:45-46).

These sick, lonely men beg Jesus for help, and He tells them to show themselves to the priests. This is a test of their faith because nothing has yet happened—they are healed because of their obedience. By Judaic law, only priests could pronounce someone "clean." A priest's approval validated a healing, and would allow the men to resume a normal life. Ten men are healed that day, but only one—the Samaritan—returned to thank Jesus, praising God.

The leprous men represent those whom Jesus has touched. Saved by His grace, we have eternal life. Transformed by His love, we are God's children. Forgiven by His mercy, we are free from sin's burden. Filled with His wisdom, we gain knowledge and understanding. Renewed by His peace, our troubled hearts can rest. Comforted by His tenderness, our sorrow turns to joy. Restored by His power, we are fully healed.

> **Think about** how Jesus spoke to the whole group, but the Samaritan heard Jesus speak to him individually. All had felt Jesus' touch, but only he knew the honor of personal fellowship with his Lord. God has touched each of us in many ways. How have we responded? Do we, like the Samaritan, praise God, thanking Him for who He is and what He has done for us? Or do we, like the nine, receive His healing and then go our way?

The Kingdom of God Personified

Anticipating a powerful, visible kingdom, the Pharisees ask Jesus when God's kingdom will come. They had seen His miracles, but He is not the type of leader they had expected. Knowing their impatience for a visible kingdom, Jesus underlines His mission. Through Jesus' life, God had repeatedly demonstrated His power before them, yet they stubbornly refused to believe.

These Old Testament scholars should have recognized Jesus as the Messiah who would establish God's kingdom. Until His kingdom is fully established, though, we can see it only by faith in what Christ has done. Nicodemus, a Pharisee, knew this (John 3:2). Now Jesus tells His disciples additional truths concerning the time the Son of Man will reappear in glory.

Christ's suffering followers will long for His return. False teachers and prophets will abound. The Son of Man's sudden, unexpected reappearance will reveal those who are faithful. His reappearance will be global; but first, certain events must occur. The Son of Man will fall into His enemies' hands and suffer humiliation and rejection. People will practice immorality as in the days of Noah (Genesis 6:11). An arrogant, materialistic society will develop, built around the gods of commerce, agriculture, and business. Jesus likens it to the age of Sodom and Gomorrah (Genesis 18:20-33; 19:24-26).

Many of these verses sound like descriptions of our highly industrialized societies. When Jesus refers to Lot's wife, who looked back while leaving Sodom to see what had been left behind (Genesis 19:32), He says, *"Whoever seeks to preserve his life will lose it, but whoever loses his life will keep it"* (Luke 17:33). As in the days of Noah, Abraham, and Jesus, many today are so concerned with their earthly possessions that they are utterly unprepared for His coming.

Replying to a question about when the Son of Man will return, Jesus uses a proverb, implying that He will appear when the situation is ripe for judgment. We do not know the exact date. We must abide in Christ so we can eagerly await that day (1 John 2:28).

During the present age, God's kingdom is spiritual, and we who believe in Jesus are its citizens. We live in a time when the world's opposition to God underlies our culture. We are really living in two worlds. The apostle Paul wrote, *"Our citizenship is in heaven, and from it we await a Savior, the Lord Jesus Christ, who will transform our lowly body to be like His glorious body"* (Philippians 3:20-21). We are called to live as citizens of heaven in a world that does not acknowledge our king. The world that opposes Christ will oppose us (John 15:18-19). We will face tension, pressures, temptations, and trials. In ourselves, we are unable to withstand such opposition, but we need not depend on ourselves. Jesus Christ is our strength (Philippians 4:13).

Personalize this lesson.

☑ As citizens of heaven in this fallen and broken world, let's make our faith evident. How can we do this? We are to be *in* this world but not *of* it. Jesus said, *"I do not ask that You take them out of the world, but that You keep them from the evil one. They are not of the world, just as I am not of the world. Sanctify them in the truth; Your word is truth. As you sent Me into the world, so I have sent them into the world. And for their sake I consecrate Myself, that they also may be sanctified in truth"* (John 17:15-19).

Jesus sends us into the world and equips us to live for Him here. He teaches us how to live for Him—by not tempting others to sin, forgiving those who offend us, trusting Him, obeying His commands as faithful servants, worshiping and thanking Him, patiently, steadfastly awaiting His coming, and being alert and prepared for His return. What will you do to represent Jesus well and to live for Him in the kingdom of God?

The Right Attitude
Luke 18

Memorize God's Word: Luke 18:17.

❖ Luke 18:1-8—The Power of Persistence

1. How would you compare the widow's request and attitude with how believers are to relate to God?

    _____

    _____

    _____

2. a. How would you explain the parable's comparison between God and the unjust judge?

    _____

    _____

    _____

    b. What is the parable's message?

    _____

    _____

❖ Luke 18:9-17—Humble Prayer

3. How is the Pharisee's behavior in the parable like that of the crowd Jesus addresses?

    _____

    _____

4. Contrast the results of the Pharisee's and tax collector's prayers.

    _____

    _____

    _____

5. Read Luke 14:7-11; 18:9-17. What is Jesus trying to teach us about prayer?

    _____

    _____

6. Why are the people bringing children to Jesus? (See also Matthew 19:13.)

    _____

    _____

7. What do the disciples do that seems out of character for them? What is their reason for doing so?

    _____

    _____

8. In what way must we be like little children to enter the kingdom of God?

    _____

    _____

❖ Luke 18:18-30—An Obstacle to Faith

9. How does the rich man show his understanding of Jesus' extraordinary qualities and his devotion to the Law?

    _____

    _____

10. In what way does Jesus allude to His oneness with God, and how does He expose the young man's real allegiance?

    _____

    _____

11. How does Jesus contrast man's power with God's?

_____

_____

12. What does Jesus say will be the results of sacrificing for the sake of the kingdom?

_____

_____

❖ Luke 18:31-34; Matthew 20:17-19—Count the Cost

13. Why does Jesus warn the disciples about the coming events? (See also Luke 14:25-33.)

_____

_____

14. Thinking back over past lessons, why is it important to count the cost of discipleship?

_____

_____

15. What will soon happen to Jesus at the hands of

a. the Jews? _____

_____

b. the Gentiles? _____

_____

c. God? _____

_____

❖ Luke 18:35-43—Faith Rewarded

16. a. What do you learn about the blind beggar from these verses, and how does Jesus respond to him?

_____

_____

b. How would you apply this story to your own life?

_____

_____

17. Why do those who are leading the crowd tell the blind man to be silent?

_____

_____

18. How does his reaction parallel the parable in verses 1-8?

_____

_____

19. How does the blind man illustrate this chapter's theme of having right attitudes?

_____

_____

Apply what you have learned. Our attitudes form the basis of what we say and do. Unlike emotions, they are an act of our will. *"Put on then, as God's chosen ones, holy and beloved, compassionate hearts, kindness, humility, meekness, and patience…. [and] love, which binds [these virtues] together in perfect harmony. And let the peace of Christ rule in your hearts, to which indeed you were called in one body. And be thankful….. whatever you do, in word or deed, do everything in the name of the Lord Jesus, giving thanks to God the Father through Him"* (Colossians 3:12-17). Will you ask God to help you develop or strengthen an attitude of humble obedience?

The Right Attitude
Luke 18

The Attitude of Persistence

Jesus' parable of the persistent widow follows His earlier warnings (17:22-37). The disciples, having heard what to expect as the time of His return draws near, may wonder if they will have the faith needed to endure such trials. We may wonder, too. World events, evil, or pain can cause even a mature Christian's faith to waver. Jesus tells this parable because, in such times, we *"ought always to pray and not lose heart"* (18:1), underscoring the importance of prayerful perseverance in our Christian walk.

In Jesus' day, King Herod and the Roman governors appointed many corrupt Gentile judges who took bribes from the Jews. The widow has no money or influence to convince the ungodly judge to act on her behalf, yet her persistence causes him to grant her request. He responds just to get rid of her. In contrast, verses 6-7 assure us of God's loving readiness to help those who call upon His name, for *"He will give justice to them speedily"* (Luke 18:8).

Think about how easy it is to trust God when things are going well, but how tempting it is to give up when they are not. We must persist in prayer, believing that—even when we see no immediate evidence—God is working out His answer to our prayers (Hebrews 10:22-23).

The Right Attitude and the Right Spirit

Some in the crowd have *"trusted in themselves that they were righteous"* (Luke 18:9), viewing themselves as better than others. Jesus tells them a parable of a Pharisee and a tax collector who go to the temple to pray. The first man stands apart from those he considers beneath him, praising himself before the Lord. What a contrast between this "righteous" Pharisee and the tax collector, who recognizes his sinfulness and need. He does just what Christ tells His disciples to do: *"When you pray, do not heap up empty phrases as the Gentiles do, for they think that they will be heard for their many words. Do not be like them, for your Father knows what you need before you ask Him"* (Matthew 6:7-8). In this parable Jesus points out man's need for genuine humility rather than self-righteousness, because God justifies repentant sinners.

The first parable teaches that we must not give up but continue to pray in faith. The second teaches that our prayers must always rest in God's character, not in ourselves. God hears and answers our prayers, not because of who we are, but because of who He is—and not because of how good we are, but because of how good He is.

To emphasize that only the truly humble will enter God's kingdom, Jesus receives the children brought to Him. The disciples consider it an intrusion, but Jesus says, *"To such belongs the kingdom of God"* (Luke 18:16). Most children display humility, faith, dependence, and trust. They naturally depend on someone stronger than themselves. God wants us to have this same attitude of trust in Him. Christ's message is clear: To enter God's kingdom we need a child's attitude—an open mind, obedience, humility, and dependence on God.

An Attitude of Stewardship

Later, a rich ruler asks Jesus a crucial question: *"What must I do to inherit eternal life?"* (18:18). When he calls Jesus *"Good teacher,"* Jesus challenges him to decide whether he truly believes Jesus is God, or is merely greeting Him politely. Knowing the man has tried hard to keep the Law, Jesus comes to the heart of the matter: *"One thing you still lack. Sell all that you have and distribute to the poor, and you will have treasure in heaven; and come, follow Me"* (18:22). He touches on the one thing that means more than God to the ruler, who is forced to acknowledge the importance money plays in his life. It is the obstacle keeping him from inheriting eternal life.

Jesus is not saying wealth is wrong, but that our attitude about it can be a problem. His hearers wonder who, then, can be saved—a question reflecting their belief that God favored the rich, so they were the most likely candidates for heaven. If they could not be saved, then who could possibly qualify? The message is clear: none can. It is impossible for man to meet God's requirements unaided. However, *"what is impossible with man is possible with God"* (18:27), who offers salvation as a gift to all who will receive it.

Peter blurts out, *"We have left our homes and followed You"* (18:28). Jesus responds that those who put Him first will be richly compensated on earth and in eternity. Trials may come as a result of following Christ, but so will blessings. This teaching is verified in Jesus' own life. Even here, He is moving steadily toward Jerusalem to face enemies who plot to crucify Him; He does not shy away from giving His own life for the sake of those in desperate spiritual need (Romans 3:23; 6:23).

Jesus tells His disciples just what He will suffer once He is *"delivered over to the Gentiles"* (Luke 18:32): He will be mocked, insulted, spat on, flogged, and killed; but *"on the third day He will rise"* (18:33). The disciples do not understand, because His meaning is *"hidden from them"* (18:34).

Faith Rewarded

In many ways, the *"blind man"* (18:35), identified as Bartimaeus in Mark 10:46, sees more clearly than those around him. When he learns that Jesus is passing by in a crowd, he seizes the moment, crying out, *"Jesus, Son of David, have mercy on me!"* (Luke 18:38). Calling the Lord *"Son of David"* shows his belief that Jesus is the Messiah and that He will have mercy on him. The crowd rebukes him, but he continues begging Jesus for help. Jesus asks, *"What do you want Me to do for you?"* (18:41). The man's answer reveals full confidence in Jesus' ability to heal him, and his faith is rewarded: Jesus instantly gives him the ability to see! Bartimaeus praises God and follows Jesus. The witnesses also give glory to God—the ultimate purpose of any miracle.

Personalize this lesson.

Our beliefs and actions cannot really be separated. They are two sides of the same coin. The poor widow in Jesus' first parable persists because she honestly believes that if she pesters the judge long enough, he will give her justice. The tax collector who knows his sinfulness goes to the temple and prays. Jesus calls the rich ruler to *"Sell all that you have"* (18:22). But he cannot do it because he lacks trust that God will provide for him. Bartimaeus displays his faith by shouting so loudly that the crowd has to give way. He is willing to face the crowd's scorn because he is utterly confident that Jesus will answer him.

We can have correct doctrine and theology, but we must believe with our hearts, and not just our heads, or we will not live consistent with our faith. Is God calling you to more consistent prayer? To more sacrificial giving? To depend on Him rather than trusting in your abilities? Ask Him to increase your faith in Him—in His faithfulness, goodness, and provision. Then begin acting on your faith in Him in whatever ways you can as He gives you opportunities.

Triumphant Journey to Jerusalem
Luke 19

Memorize God's Word: Luke 19:38.

❖ Luke 19:1-10—Zacchaeus Meets Jesus

1. What does Zacchaeus's climbing the tree indicate to you about his inner need?

2. What does Jesus' response to Zacchaeus reveal about His knowledge of and response to our needs?

3. How do the crowd and Jesus differ in their responses to a sinner?

4. How does Zacchaeus express true repentance?

5. In Luke 19:9, why does Jesus call Zacchaeus a *"son of Abraham"*? (See also Galatians 3:7.)

6. How does Jesus' encounter with Zacchaeus exemplify Luke
    19:10?

    _____

    _____

7. Compare Zacchaeus to the rich ruler from Luke 18:18-23 with
    regard to their

	Zacchaeus	The rich young ruler
Social position		
National heritage		
Ethics		
Response to Jesus		

❖ Luke 19:11-27—The Nobleman and His Servants

8. What is Jesus' purpose in telling this parable?

    _____

    _____

9. Where does the nobleman go, and why does he go there?

    _____

    _____

10. What does the nobleman do, and what are his instructions
    before he departs?

    _____

    _____

11. Who do the nobleman, the citizens, and the servants represent?

    _____

    _____

12. Why does the nobleman condemn the third servant so severely?

_____

_____

13. What spiritual principle is illustrated in verses 24-26?

_____

_____

14. Read verse 13 with verses 24-26. What has the Lord given you to steward for Him? How are you doing with it?

_____

_____

❖ Luke 19:28-40—The Triumphal Entry

15. Where is Jesus going, and why is His use of a donkey to get there important? (See also Zechariah 9:9; Matthew 21:1-5.)

_____

_____

16. How do the disciples express their personal love and care for Jesus as His journey begins?

_____

_____

❖ Luke 19:41-48—Jesus in Jerusalem

17. What is God's attitude toward sinners as exemplified in these verses?

_____

_____

18. What sin does Jesus ascribe to Jerusalem and what consequences will follow?

_____

_____

19. What is Jesus' reaction when He enters the temple? (See also Mark 11:15-17.)

_____

_____

20. As a result of His ministry within the temple, how do the people's responses differ?

_____

_____

21. How would you describe Jesus' character as revealed in Luke 19?

_____

_____

Apply what you have learned. Jerusalem fell because she did not *"know the time of* [her] *visitation"* (19:44). Christians experience each day as the time of God's coming. *"Now is the favorable time; behold, now is the day of salvation"* (2 Corinthians 6:2). What opportunities is God offering you today? What temptations are you facing today? God will visit you now if you invite Him into your circumstances. Where do you need His help? Ask Him for it.

Triumphant Journey to Jerusalem
Luke 19

Salvation Comes to a Sinner's House

Zacchaeus is the chief tax collector in prosperous Jericho; he works for Rome and cheats his fellow Jews, who, not surprisingly, hate him. Zacchaeus is curious about Jesus, and because the crowd is large and he is short, he climbs a sycamore tree to wait for Jesus' arrival. Jesus' loving response to this outcast results in Zacchaeus receiving Him into his heart and home.

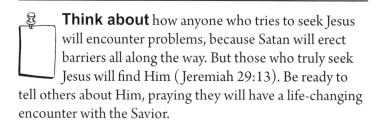

Think about how anyone who tries to seek Jesus will encounter problems, because Satan will erect barriers all along the way. But those who truly seek Jesus will find Him (Jeremiah 29:13). Be ready to tell others about Him, praying they will have a life-changing encounter with the Savior.

As Jesus enters Zacchaeus's home, people murmur. They know this man is a sinner, but they fail to see their own sinfulness. Jesus' visit changes Zacchaeus, who follows his profession of faith with radical action. Unlike the rich ruler (Luke 18:22-23), Zacchaeus sees his new relationship with Christ and his good standing with God as more valuable than earthly wealth. Jesus assures him that *"salvation has come to this house"* (19:9). He takes the initiative to reach out and does not preach to Zacchaeus, but meets him as a friend. Typically, this friendship with sinners offends the crowd because they do not understand God's unconditional love.

The King's Servant

Nearing Jerusalem, Jesus tells a parable to explain His kingdom, and to show what God expects of His people until Christ's return. A nobleman, leaving to be declared king, gives 10 servants one mina (three month's wages) each to invest until he returns. The nobleman represents Jesus: He, too, will go away (die, then rise and ascend) to return as King. The Lord charges us, like the servants, to make use of what He gives us— salvation by faith in Christ. We are to share the gospel with others so that God's kingdom multiplies. This priceless gift is meant to accrue a greater return for God, who invested in us. We are to do this, like the servants in the parable, among citizens who refuse to be subject to their true ruler.

The nobleman returns as king and asks his servants about their investment of what he had given them. The first earned 10 minas and is charged with care for 10 cities. The second earned five and is given care of five cities. The third says he feared the king's wrath, so he hid the money. The consequences he suffers illustrate a spiritual law that is also true in the physical realm. Our grasp of spiritual truth grows or diminishes according to how much we exercise it. When we put our spiritual knowledge to work, we gain more light. God does not expect us to obey Him in our own strength; His life in us will be fruitful (John 15:4-5). There will be a day of judgment when all who ignored God's call to repent will be banished forever (Revelation 20:11-15). The Lord is merciful, but He will not force anyone to have a relationship with Him. Those who go into darkness do so because they have chosen a path that leads away from Jesus.

A Triumphal Entry Into Jerusalem

On His way to Jerusalem, Jesus nears Bethany—the village where Mary, Martha, and Lazarus live. He tells two disciples to bring Him a colt. As they untie one, its owner asks the reason; they explain, and take it away unopposed. Christ's riding on a colt as He enters Jerusalem fulfills Zechariah 9:9. Donkeys were highly regarded in that culture. Traditionally, kings sat astride horses if they entered a territory intending to make war, but rode on donkeys if they came in peace. As Jesus enters Jerusalem for the last time before His crucifixion, He demonstrates by riding on a colt that He is coming in peace as their King.

The crowd rejoices as Jesus enters the city. For the first time He seems to fulfill their dream, and they praise God, fulfilling Psalm 118:26-27.

Religious leaders, who supposedly knew the Scriptures, should have anticipated their Messiah's arrival and recognized the prophecy that was being fulfilled in their midst. Instead, their reaction to this celebration is to order Jesus to quiet everyone. Their pride and self-righteousness have hardened into hatred. Having seen His miracles and heard His preaching, they are unable to find any sin in Jesus. Still, they reject Him.

Jesus Is Tender Yet Firm

Seeing Jerusalem, Jesus weeps over its future destruction. This event will occur because the people *"did not know the time of your visitation"* (Luke 19:44)—a prophecy fulfilled in AD 70, when the Romans leveled the city. He then takes harsh action at the temple. Some merchants are using prescribed religious festivals to get rich—a practice that would be impossible without the religious leaders' cooperation. Israelites making an offering at the temple are obliged to use a certain type of currency, prompting enterprising money changers to set up shop in the temple's courtyard. Livestock sellers and dove vendors fill the courtyard, selling expensive animals, the only ones the priests approve as sacrificial offerings. Prices are far beyond the normal rate outside the temple, prompting Jesus to say that they had made His *"house of prayer"* a *"den of robbers."* (19:46).

We have seen an illustration of the Lord's sternness toward lazy, unproductive servants. Now we see, in His cleansing of the temple, a symbolic act foreshadowing the final judgment to come. People who commit themselves to honoring God, yet victimize and cheat the poor, stand in danger of greater judgment than those outside the kingdom who do similar things. There is always the chance that outsiders—like Zacchaeus—will repent. But a religious person who gives a nod to what is right and then acts dishonestly is sternly condemned. The Pharisees not only overcharge the helpless poor God places in their care, but do so blatantly in the temple—a place dedicated to worship.

Personalize this lesson.

✓ Did you notice that even though the three servants in Luke 19:11-27 all had the same master, their perceptions of their master were very different? The third servant viewed his master as "a severe man." Because he was afraid of his master, he hid his master's money instead of investing it for a return.

How does your perception of your Master, Jesus, affect the way you love and serve Him? Are you confident of His love, grace, and goodness toward you so you can relax as you serve Him with joy? Or are you afraid that He is watching for you to make a mistake so He can punish you? Ask God to give you an accurate perception of who He is so that you can love and serve Him with freedom and confidence.

Jesus and the Religious Leaders
Luke 20

❖ **Luke 20:1-8; Review 19:45-48—Jesus' Authority Is Questioned**

1. What is Jesus doing in the temple?

   _____

   _____

   _____

2. What is the motive behind the religious leaders' question regarding Jesus' authority?

   _____

   _____

   _____

3. Why does Jesus answer them with a question, and how does He use their reply to answer their original question?

   _____

   _____

   _____

4. What principles for witnessing can we learn from Jesus' encounter with the religious leaders?

   _____

   _____

   _____

❖ Luke 20:9-18—The Parable of the Vineyard and the Tenants

5.   Read this parable with Matthew 21:43, and Hebrews 1:1-3. Who do the vineyard owner, the servants, the beloved son, and the tenants represent?

_____

_____

_____

6.   How do the tenants respond to (a) the servants ? (b) the son ?

_____

_____

7.   a.   Read 1 Peter 2:6-8. What are some of the ways Jesus is described, directly and indirectly?

_____

_____

   b.   Why do unbelievers stumble on Jesus, the Rock?

_____

_____

❖ Luke 20:19-26—A Plot to Trap Jesus

8.   How do the spies sent by the religious leaders describe Jesus?

_____

_____

9.   Is their description accurate? Please explain your answer.

_____

_____

10. a.   What is the point of their question in verse 22?

_____

_____

    b.   How would you apply Jesus' answer to your life today?

_____

_____

❖ Luke 20:27-40—Resurrection and Marriage

11. Sadducees are the priestly aristocrats—very political and materialistic. They do not believe in the resurrection or life after death. Why does Jesus warn against them? (See also Matthew 16:11-12.)

_____

_____

12. Considering the Sadducees' views on the resurrection, why do they pose such a question to Jesus in verses 28-33?

_____

_____

13. How does Jesus refute the Sadducees' beliefs and also offer truth about those resurrected in the Lord?

_____

_____

❖ Luke 20:41-47—Who Is the Christ?

14. How do the people relate the Christ with David?

_____

_____

15. In the psalm Jesus quotes, how does David relate himself to the Christ? Explain how both these descriptions are true.

_____

_____

_____

_____

16. Why does Jesus warn His disciples against the teachers of the Law, and what is the consequence of their actions?

_____

_____

17. What is the outcome for people who reject Jesus? (See also Luke 19:41-44.)

_____

_____

18. a. Why does Jesus publicly expose the chief priests, teachers of Law, and Sadducees?

_____

_____

b. How do Jesus' attitude and statements to them challenge you?

_____

_____

Apply what you have learned. Our lesson has shown us the power of Jesus' wisdom. As believers in Christ, we need not worry how we will respond in the midst of spiritual opposition. He who lives within us will teach us, *"for the Holy Spirit will teach you in that very hour what you ought to say"* (Luke 12:12). Is there a relationship in your life in which you feel inadequate to speak spiritual truth with Christ-like grace? Don't let fear keep you from engaging. Ask God for help, wait on Him until He gives it, and then go into that situation with confidence in Him.

Jesus and the Religious Leaders
Luke 20

As Jews gather in Jerusalem to celebrate Passover, religious leaders increasingly confront Jesus in order to discredit Him. Yet they do not want to start a riot, costing them their privileged positions. Jesus continues to teach and preach—despite their questioning of His authority. In fact, Jesus replies with a question of His own: Was John's baptism from heaven or from men (Luke 20:3)? John the Baptist first proclaimed Jesus as the *"Lamb of God, who takes away the sin of the world"* (John 1:29). The leaders had rejected John's message but will not say so because many Jews accept John as God's prophet and Jesus as God's Messiah. If they say John is not God's prophet, they will cause an uproar. If they say he is, they will have to admit Jesus is the Christ. They refuse to answer either way. Consequently, Jesus refuses to answer them.

Jesus exposes the religious leaders' true attitudes when He shares the parable of the tenants. Absentee landlords rented out much of Israel's land to tenant farmers. These landlords sent servants to collect a portion of the harvest as the landlord's share. In this parable, the vineyard owner represents God. The tenants symbolize those called to share the ministry of His kingdom—as represented by the Jewish religious leaders. The servants represent all the prophets—including John the Baptist—whom the leaders have rejected. The beloved son represents God's Son, Jesus Christ. By sending servant after servant, and finally his beloved son, the merciful landlord gives the rebellious tenants many chances to respond correctly. But they refuse—and mistreat the servants.

In Jesus' day, tenants could put in a claim to the property if a landowner died leaving no heir. In this parable, the tenants assume the owner is dead. They think by killing the heir, they can claim the land. But God will justly punish those who have demonstrated such evil behavior against His Son. God's mercy and judgment are two sides of the same coin: Those who reject His mercy will receive His judgment. Jesus quotes Psalm 118:22: *"The stone that the builders rejected has become the cornerstone."* The *"stone"* they refuse to accept is Jesus, the Christ. They will suffer terrible punishment as a result of rejecting Him.

Scribes and priests know Jesus' parable points at them. They want the Roman authorities to arrest Him, so they send spies who try to trap Him by asking a sly question about paying Roman taxes. Caesar's image was stamped on each coin in his domain. He required all adults under his rule to pay him taxes with these coins. Although a small tax, to the Jews—who refused to acknowledge any king other than God—it was humiliating and implied acceptance of Caesar as their king. However, these same religious leaders charged a fee for converting Roman money into temple coins. They profited from the Roman government while they complained about it. Jesus asks for a Roman coin and points to Caesar's image on it. His words, *"'Render to Caesar the things that are Caesar's, and to God the things that are God's'"* (Luke 20:25), imply that because Caesar had the coin minted and stamped with his image, he has the right to impose a tax on the user of that coin. Likewise, because God created humanity in His image (Genesis 1:26), He has the right to exercise authority over all people. Jesus is actually saying that people have dual citizenship. They should show proper respect to God—the ultimate authority of their lives—and to Caesar, the civil authority of their day (1 Peter 2:17).

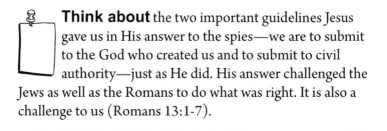

Think about the two important guidelines Jesus gave us in His answer to the spies—we are to submit to the God who created us and to submit to civil authority—just as He did. His answer challenged the Jews as well as the Romans to do what was right. It is also a challenge to us (Romans 13:1-7).

The Sadducees—a Jewish sect made up of politically powerful and wealthy priests—accepted the Law but did not believe in angels, spirits, or resurrection of the dead. Although the various religious groups were at odds with one another, they were united in opposing Jesus. As others fail to trap Jesus into making a mistake, the Sadducees try by asking Jesus about the marriage law (Deuteronomy 25:5). This law said that if a man died without heirs, his brother had to marry the widow and raise children in the dead man's name. Perhaps the Sadducees think they will prove themselves right if Jesus is unable to answer. Instead, Jesus addresses the real problem—the Sadducees' unbelief. Doubt causes them to wrongly think the resurrection life is bound by the same limits as earthly life.

Our bodies will be totally transformed after we die. After His resurrection, Jesus was recognizable. He ate, He could walk through closed doors (John 20:19, 26), change His appearance, and even vanish (Luke 24:15-16, 30-31). From these facts, believers conclude that we will recognize each other and do similar things. Scripture says death will end, resulting in no need for marriage and procreation.

After revealing the foolishness of their question, Jesus uses a portion of the Old Testament the Sadducees accept as true, to prove the resurrection of the dead. In Exodus, God declares that He is—present tense—*"the God of Abraham and the God of Isaac and the God of Jacob."* It would not make sense for God to call Himself the God of the dead. Those who believe in the Resurrection praise Jesus' answer. No one dares to ask Him any more questions.

Jesus now questions the leaders. Referring to Psalm 110:1, He asks, if the Messiah comes from David's line, why does David humbly acknowledge his own offspring as Lord? If David does, the scribes and Pharisees— who have seen Jesus' power—should be humble enough to do the same. Jesus exposes the religious leaders' hypocrisy, warning the people against teachers who take advantage of defenseless people and prefer admiration over God's truth and approval. Jesus warns, *"They will receive the greater condemnation"* (Luke 20:47).

Personalize this lesson.

The religious leaders hated Jesus. Why did these genuinely religious men fail to recognize their Messiah? Being religious is no guarantee of being right. Worse yet, a religious attitude can lead to deadly pride.

Anything—any ambition, or situation, or project, or lifestyle—that becomes more important than loving and knowing God is dangerous. Paul, a former Pharisee, wrote after becoming a follower of Christ, *"Whatever gain I had, I counted as loss for the sake of Christ. Indeed, I count everything as loss because of the surpassing worth of knowing Christ Jesus my Lord"* (Philippians 3:7-8). Ask God to reveal any spiritual pride that may be hidden in your heart. Do you feel self-righteous because of your Bible study or memorization, your charitable deeds and giving, your church involvement, or any other religious attitudes or activities? Confess these to God. Ask Him to give you a truly humble heart that values knowing and loving Him more than any praise.

Jerusalem and Christ's Return
Luke 21

Memorize God's Word: Luke 12:40.

❖ Luke 21:1-9—The Spirit of Giving

1. What connection do you see between Luke 20:45-47 and Luke 21:1-4?

    _____

    _____

    _____

2. Why does Jesus say the poor widow gave *"more than all of them"* (21:3)?

    _____

    _____

3. The temple is described as being *"adorned with noble stones and offerings"* (21:5). What does Jesus prophesy about the temple?

    _____

    _____

    _____

4. What events will occur just before this prophecy is fulfilled?

    _____

    _____

    _____

5. What attitudes are Christians to avoid while facing disaster or persecution?

   _____

   _____

❖ Luke 21:10-19—Signs For the End of the Age

6. Jesus claims that natural disasters and fearful political events are coming (21:10-11). Before these disasters begin, what events must occur?

   _____

   _____

7. Why are the disciples not to worry about how to answer their accusers?

   _____

   _____

8. How can we apply the promise of verse 15 to our lives (See also 1 Corinthians 1:30; James 1:5.)

   _____

   _____

   _____

9. After the warning in verse 16, what does the promise in verse 18 mean?

   _____

   _____

   _____

❖ Luke 21:20-28—Persecutions and Natural Disasters

10. What does Jesus prophesy about Jerusalem and its inhabitants?

   _____

   _____

11. a. How will people know Jerusalem's destruction is about to occur?

_____

_____

    b. What are they to do?

_____

_____

12. Why are Christ's followers to be encouraged at such a time?

_____

_____

13. Does this passage frighten or encourage you? Why?

_____

_____

_____

❖ Luke 21:29-38—The Parable of the Fig Tree

14. How does Jesus use the fig tree to teach about spiritual awareness and assurance?

_____

_____

15. Why does Jesus say those alive at the day of His return must be prayerful and constantly alert?

_____

_____

16. How can guarding against distraction and having an expectant attitude help us as we await Jesus' return?

_____

_____

_____

17. Jesus knows He is facing betrayal, trial, and crucifixion. How does His behavior in these last days serve as an example for us?

_____

_____

❖ Review of Prophecies Regarding Jerusalem and Jesus' Return

18. How do Jesus' words in verses 8-36

     a.   equip you to know the signs of His return?

        _____

        _____

     b.   enable you to cope with present difficulties?

        _____

        _____

     c.   encourage you to both prepare and look forward to His coming?

        _____

        _____

Apply what you have learned. Jesus' prophecies about the end times have two aspects for believers. They assure us of His power and help while warning of persecutions and trials. Are we mature enough to accept the warnings as well as the assurance of His help? Are we honest enough to accept the reality that following Jesus brings difficulties as well as blessings? What are some important steps you can take to be better prepared for difficulties?

Jerusalem and Christ's Return
Luke 21

Moses instructed the people, *"You shall not harden your heart or shut your hand against your poor brother, but you shall open your hand to him and lend him sufficient for his need, whatever it may be"* (Deuteronomy 15:7-8). The Jews were required to *"bring the full tithe* [a 10th of their goods] *into the storehouse"* (Malachi 3:10). These gifts supported the priests, who in turn used them to help the needy. Because of these laws, many religious leaders lived very well—sometimes at others' expense.

Sacrificial Giving

Jesus often warns His disciples about teachers of the Law. They appear pious, but *"devour widows' houses"* (Luke 20:47). Here, the disciples watch the wealthy put their donations into the temple treasury. Afterward, a poor widow puts in two tiny coins. Jesus says she *"has put in more than all of them"* (21:3). We may be deceived when we see things only as they appear. Jesus sees the widow's heart and knows that her gift—in proportion to what she has—is enormous. Meanwhile, the rich, who give out of their wealth, are actually being stingy.

We are to give in order to please God, not to impress others. Otherwise, the honor we get from people is the only reward we will ever receive. Jesus said, *"When you give to the needy ... do not let your left hand know what your right hand is doing, so that your giving may be in secret. And your Father who sees in secret will reward you"* (Matthew 6:2-4).

 Think about how we can honor God as the source and provider of all we possess by giving a portion back to Him. Our giving is an act of worship—an obvious way to demonstrate our love for God and our gratitude. Therefore, *"each one must give as he has decided in his heart, not reluctantly or under compulsion, for God loves a cheerful giver"* (2 Corinthians 9:7).

Devastation and Destruction

The disciples express their admiration of the temple's beauty. Shocked to hear Jesus prophesy its destruction, they question Him. Jesus responds by referring to the end of the age. He warns that many false christs will come. The Jews were expecting a political Messiah who would liberate them from Rome. This expectation made them easy prey for teachers who proclaimed this misleading message. Jesus, the true Christ, states that war will come before the temple falls. Historical records reveal bloody revolts took place from AD 63-70. Jewish Zealots occupied the temple in AD 68 until the Romans leveled it in AD 70, causing the Christians to flee. Jesus had predicted this event (Luke 19:43-44). After the fall of Jerusalem in AD 73, some Zealots remained at the Jewish fortress at Masada. When surrounded by Romans, the Jews inside chose to commit mass suicide rather than surrender. Jesus warns His disciples of coming persecutions. The book of Acts records some of these trials and tells of the Holy Spirit helping the disciples respond to their persecutors—just as Jesus promises.

Much (or all, depending on one's interpretation) of Jesus' prophecy concerning future events was fulfilled at the fall of Jerusalem. He also predicts that wars, disasters, starvation, epidemics, and *"great signs from heaven"* (21:11) will come before the end times. He concludes the prophecy by saying, *"They will fall by the edge of the sword and be led captive among all nations, and Jerusalem will be trampled underfoot by the Gentiles, until the times of the Gentiles are fulfilled"* (Luke 21:24). The *"times of the Gentiles"* refer to the time Jerusalem will be placed in Gentile hands—sometimes by force—starting from Israel's first exile by Nebuchadnezzar until Christ's Second Coming.

Watch and Pray

Before Jesus returns, an increase in natural disasters will cause great fear. Jesus does not mention these final events to frighten people. His purpose is to encourage believers to stay alert. It is easy to grow careless about God's kingdom and become busy in worldly affairs. Yet His disciples are to *"straighten up and raise your heads, because your redemption is drawing near"* (21:28). What terrifies the world should not terrify believers. The end of this age means the beginning of the new age.

Jesus then tells the parable of the fig tree—explaining that when fig trees sprout leaves, we know spring has come and summer is on the way. Similarly, we can expect the coming of God's kingdom when we see the signs of the times. Jesus continues, *"Truly, I say to you, this generation will not pass away until all has taken place. Heaven and earth will pass away, but My words will not pass away"* (21:32-33). There are two ways to understand the phrase *"this generation will not pass away."* The word *generation* means the whole group of people born and living at the same time. This could mean that the Jews, as a people, will not pass away and will be there when the age ends and the Lord returns. It could also mean that the people who actually see these things take place will also live to see the Lord return.

Each generation of Christians eagerly waits for the Lord's return (Hebrews 9:28). His coming is 2,000 years closer than it was for 1st-century believers. Jesus' warning about keeping watch (Luke 21:34-36) is still relevant. We do not know when He will return. As we look at our own generation, we see the very things Jesus warned His disciples to watch out for.

God's children should be alert and watchful—faithful to our appointed tasks. We do not need to try to discover the secrets of God's plan. While we can recognize the general season of His second coming, we do not need to waste time guessing the specifics. Even Jesus, while on earth, did not know exactly when He would return (Matthew 24:36-37). We are assured only that the Lord *is* coming—knowing this should make a difference in our lives. The best we can do is follow the example of Jesus, who, after saying all these things and knowing He would be crucified, continued teaching daily in the temple.

Personalize this lesson.

✓ Christians have different interpretations of Jesus' words about Jerusalem's destruction, and such differences sometimes lead to heated discussions. But remember that Jesus' discussion of Jerusalem's destruction fits into a bigger context. Jesus had just warned His listeners about wealthy scribes who *"devour widows' houses,"* and then pointed out the poor widow who gave *"more than all of them."* The primary lesson here is not about trials or end-time events; the primary lesson is about having genuine love for God and our neighbors. Take some time to ponder deeply how love for God and your neighbors—and God's great love for you—overrides any need to worry about the future.

Lesson 27

The Lord's Supper
Luke 22:1-30

❖ Luke 22:1-6—Judas Agrees to Betray Jesus

1. Read Luke 22:1 and Exodus 12:21-28. Regarding the first Passover observance,

   a. how do the people respond to God's instructions?

   _____

   _____

   b. how does God respond to His people?

   _____

   _____

2. Judas Iscariot, one of the 12 disciples, holds their money bag and offerings. How does he abuse his position of trust? (See also John 12:4-6.)

   _____

   _____

   _____

3. Read 1 Timothy 6:10. Considering his close association with Jesus, why is Judas still open to Satan's presence and power?

   _____

   _____

   _____

4. From your own knowledge of human nature, what motives other than greed or lust for money can cause people to be untrue to Jesus Christ?

    _____

    _____

❖ Luke 22:7-13—Preparations for the Passover

5. What special foods are prepared for the Passover? (See also Exodus 12:5, 8.)

    _____

    _____

6. In Luke 22, we see Peter and John preparing the Passover meal. Where do they prepare it?

    _____

    _____

7. Why or why wouldn't the disciples sense something unusual about Jesus and this particular Passover celebration?

    _____

    _____

    _____

8. As we seek to serve Jesus, what can we learn from Peter and John's example?

    _____

    _____

❖ Luke 22:14-18—The Passover Meal

9. In what ways does Jesus Christ fulfill the Passover? (See also John 1:29; 1 Corinthians 5:7.)

    _____

    _____

    _____

10. a. From John 13:1-16, what does Jesus know about coming events?

_____

_____

    b. With this in mind, how would you describe Jesus' attitude and actions? (See also Philippians 2:5-8.)

_____

_____

    c. How do Jesus' statements in John 13:13-16 affect your concept of service?

_____

_____

❖ Luke 22:19-23—The Last Supper

11. In the disciples' Passover meal, what does the broken bread signify?

_____

_____

12. Read 1 Corinthians 11:23-32 where Paul explains how Christians should celebrate the Lord's Supper. Why are they instructed to do so?

_____

_____

13. How does Jesus reveal that He recognizes His betrayer's identity and future?

_____

_____

14. How might your reaction have been similar to the disciples'?

_____

_____

❖ Luke 22:24-30—A Picture of True Greatness

15. How would you explain the meaning of Jesus' statements in verses 25-27?

_____

_____

16. How do you explain Jesus' words of assurance in verses 28-30 after His statements in verses 25-27?

_____

_____

17. a. How does Jesus say the disciples will be rewarded (Luke 22:30)?

_____

_____

    b. How does this apply to believers today?

_____

_____

Apply what you have learned. The Lord's Supper is as necessary for our spiritual health as a balanced diet is for our physical health. As believers share in it, we are fed spiritually and demonstrate before God, each other, and the world that we belong to Christ. Formal communion in a gathering of believers is important, and so also is regular, one-to-one communion with the Lord. Do you need to make any changes in order to make both kinds of communication a more regular and meaningful part of your spiritual life? Share your answer with a friend who can pray with you about this.

The Lord's Supper
Luke 22:1-30

Opposition and Betrayal

The Passover celebrates the Israelites' deliverance from slavery in
Egypt. God warned that all firstborn sons in Egypt would die. He told
His people to sacrifice a lamb and paint its blood on their doorframes.
God promised to spare (pass over) these homes (Exodus 12:21-36).
In Jesus' day, Jewish pilgrims annually went to Jerusalem to celebrate
the Passover. They gave thanks to God for saving the Israelites from the
fatal plague in Egypt. The seven-day Feast of Unleavened Bread, which
follows Passover, symbolizes a total cleansing from sin. It was, and is, a
time of reflection and dedication.

On the Passover week, recorded in Luke 21, 250,000 to 2 million Jews
fill Jerusalem. Meanwhile, religious leaders plot to kill Jesus. Judas—the
thieving treasurer among the disciples (John 12:4-6)—offers to help.
His motive might have been greed, jealousy, pride, or even lack of interest
in serving a "losing cause." Judas—like everyone—had a choice. Satan
tempted and ultimately controlled him. The devil has no power over those
who resist him (James 4:7). The disciples, sensing their own potential for
good or evil, ask each other which of them will betray the Lord.

The Lord's Supper

Jesus faithfully observed all Jewish festivals (Luke 2:41; John 2:13; 5:1).
Here, He sends Peter and John ahead with exact directions for preparing
His last Passover meal. The two find a man carrying a water pot (work
usually done by women). They follow him to a house and tell the
homeowner that Jesus needs his guest room to celebrate Passover. The
owner shows them a large, furnished upper room—typical of those used
by rabbis to talk openly to their followers. During the meal in this upper

room, Jesus prophesies His betrayal, humiliation, and crucifixion—as well as the future celebration of the Lord's Supper in God's kingdom.

The Passover ritual begins with a prayer of thanksgiving, followed by the first cup of wine (Luke 22:17-18). Participants also eat bitter herbs as a reminder of the Israelites' painful slavery in Egypt; unleavened bread reminds the Hebrew people of their quick departure (Exodus 12:8, 39). When the youngest son asks, *"What do you mean by this service?"* the head of the house replies, *"It is the sacrifice of the Lord's Passover"* (Exodus 12:26-27). Perhaps a disciple asks this question here. Jesus then says of the bread, *"This is My body, which is given for you. Do this in remembrance of Me"* (Luke 22:19). In doing so, He institutes a new meaning to this memorial feast now known as the Lord's Supper, Communion, or the Eucharist.

Jesus then takes the cup and says, *"This cup that is poured out for you is the new covenant in My blood"* (22:20). Blood as a symbol of cleansing, protection, and atonement was a familiar concept in Old Testament Judaism (Exodus 12:7, 12-13; Leviticus 16:11-19). The New Testament points out that sacrificial shedding of innocent blood symbolized and foreshadowed Christ's bloodshed on the cross (Hebrews 9:11-12). He suffered God's righteous penalty for our sin, fulfilling the prophecy in Isaiah 53:5: *"He was pierced for our transgressions; He was crushed for our iniquities; upon Him was the chastisement that brought us peace, and with His wounds we are healed."*

Despite their familiarity with the Passover and the symbolic use of blood, the disciples are upset. They do not understand Jesus' prediction of His suffering and death—or how it relates to Passover. They still expect Him to establish God's kingdom, and they want to share in its glory. The disciples' confusion is obvious as they are soon arguing about who will be the greatest. Only after the Resurrection are their doubts and misunderstandings resolved.

Think about how the Lord's Supper should remind us of its purpose—to *"proclaim the Lord's death until He comes"* (1 Corinthians 11:26). We express Communion, one of our highest acts of spiritual worship, through common physical acts—eating and drinking. Through taking on human flesh, Jesus brought

us salvation and sanctification. His coming to earth
demonstrates the continuity between the physical and the
spiritual (Colossians 3:23-24).

A Picture of True Greatness

John 13:3-17 gives a more complete picture of the events that happen
during the last supper. While the disciples foolishly argue over the top
positions in God's kingdom, Jesus lays aside His garments, picks up a
towel and a basin of water, and washes their feet. He teaches them—and
us—that true greatness is expressed in a life of service. Jesus instructs the
disciples to serve each other as He has served them. He then graciously
grants them a kingdom and promises rewards because they have stood
by Him in His trials. Our reward is also implied. If we "stand by Jesus" in
this life, we have the promise of everlasting life in His presence.

The symbolism of Jesus washing the disciples' feet means more than
an example of humble service to others. In John 13:8, Jesus tells Peter
to submit to His cleansing, or Peter will have no part with Him. Jesus
is referring to cleansing from sin, which will be provided through His
death on the cross. Without accepting this cleansing from the Lord, no
one can have fellowship with Him. Inner cleansing happens when we
ask for His forgiveness and are born into God's family. Jesus also speaks
of the necessity for continued cleansing from sin even after our initial
salvation experience: *"The one who has bathed does not need to wash,
except for his feet, but is completely clean"* (John 13:10). We *"wash our feet"*
by confessing our sins (1 John 1:9).

This world's system directly opposes God's system. Our own sinful
nature and Satan himself tempt us to disobey God. Until we arrive in
heaven, we will at times "get our feet dirty." As we learn to depend on the
Holy Spirit, and obey 1 John 1:9, our fellowship with the Lord will be
broken less often. *"Walk by the Spirit, and you will not gratify the desires
of the flesh.... If we live by the Spirit, let us also keep in step with the Spirit"*
(Galatians 5:16-25).

Personalize this lesson.

☑ Think for a moment about your personal definition of greatness. Does it involve humble service to others? Ask God to work His truth of greatness deep into your soul. Then look for quiet ways you can "wash the feet" of your family members, co-workers, or neighbors.

Lesson 28

Testing and Suffering
Luke 22:31-71

Memorize God's Word: Luke 22:42.

❖ Luke 22:31-38—Jesus Predicts Peter's Denial

1. How would you describe Peter's statement in verse 33?

   _____

   _____

2. What does this episode tell you about Jesus' knowledge of your sins and failures?

   _____

   _____

   _____

❖ Luke 22:39-46—Jesus Prays on the Mountain

3. What temptation does Jesus warn His disciples against in verse 40?

   _____

   _____

4. What does the disciples' falling asleep indicate about their ability to withstand temptation?

   _____

   _____

   _____

5. When Jesus prays at Gethsemane on the Mount of Olives, what is the *"cup"* (22:42) He prays to have removed from Him?

    _____

    _____

6. a. Considering Jesus' oneness with the Father, discuss His words, *"Not My will, but Yours, be done"* (22:42).

        _____

        _____

    b. How is this prayer relevant in your life?

        _____

        _____

        _____

❖ Luke 22:47-53; Matthew 26:47-56—Jesus Is Arrested

7. A crowd accompanies Judas to the garden. What are they are carrying?

    _____

    _____

8. Why do so many people accompany Judas?

    _____

    _____

9. Think about Judas's words, actions and state of mind. How is he given a chance, even now, to repent?

    _____

    _____

10. How does Jesus indicate that He is in control of the situation?

    _____

    _____

❖ Luke 22:54-62—Peter Denies Jesus

11. Read Matthew 26:57; John 11:45-53.

    a. How would you describe Caiaphas?

       _____

       _____

    b. Considering the late hour, how would you describe this meeting of priests, scribes, and elders?

       _____

       _____

12. What happens to the disciples? (See Matthew 26:56.)

    _____

    _____

13. How would you describe Peter's denials of Jesus?

    _____

    _____

    _____

14. What happens immediately after Peter's third denial?

    _____

    _____

15. Why does Peter react as he does?

    _____

    _____

❖ Luke 22:63-71—Jesus Before the Sanhedrin

16. Where is Jesus taken after His examination at the high priest's home?

    _____

    _____

17. Is the council's request legitimate (22:67)? Please give reasons for your answer.

_____

_____

_____

_____

18. How does Jesus' response expose His questioners' true motives?

_____

_____

_____

_____

Apply what you have learned. Our salvation cost Jesus not only His life, given on the cross, but also extreme humiliation and abuse from people. Do you feel slighted or offended about something? Remember Jesus' forbearance: *"If you are insulted for the name of Christ, you are blessed, because the Spirit of glory and of God rests upon you"* (1 Peter 4:14). Give your hurt and offended feelings to Jesus. Ask Him to heal your heart and give you peace so you can respond to offenses as He did.

Testing and Suffering
Luke 22:31-71

Jesus Predicts Peter's Denial

After His last Passover meal, Jesus confronts yet another disciple who will fail Him. He warns Peter of Satan's plan to *"sift"* him (22:31), but Peter is sure he will not fall. Jesus knows Peter will deny Him before dawn, but still reassures him. Throughout their earthly ministry, the disciples' needs are met. Now, Christ says they must equip themselves. He does not mean the disciples should use weapons, because He later rebukes Peter for using his sword (John 18:10). Jesus refers to Isaiah 53:12 as a prophecy about the Messiah. He knows who He is and what will happen to Him—yet He continues to trust God the Father to fulfill His purpose through His death.

Jesus in Prayer

At night, Jesus goes with His disciples to His special place of prayer— Gethsemane, a garden on the Mount of Olives. The Son of Man needs the Father's support at this crucial hour. Though Christ is God, He is also fully human (Hebrews 2:14-17; Philippians 2:5-8). While He struggles in prayer, the disciples fall asleep, *"sleeping for sorrow"* (Luke 22:45). They have a desperate need to pray. But, as Jesus says, *"The spirit indeed is willing, but the flesh is weak"* (Matthew 26:41).

Jesus' Betrayal and Arrest

Judas knows Jesus often prays at Gethsemane. He leads a hired mob to the spot, and betrays Jesus with a kiss. Peter then becomes angry and cuts off the ear of Malchus, the high priest's servant. Jesus stops to heal Malchus with a touch. The miracle seems to have no effect on the mob. They seize Jesus and take Him to the high priest's home. The fearful disciples forsake Jesus and flee (Matthew 26:56).

Think about how Jesus—even at the time of His betrayal—called Judas *"friend"* (Matthew 26:50). Judas returned the money to those who paid him, saying, *"I have sinned by betraying innocent blood"* (Matthew 27:4) before hanging himself. Judas is a tragic figure not only because he betrayed Jesus, but because he didn't turn to the One who could have lifted his hopelessness. He would have received forgiveness if he had asked Jesus for it. How sad that Judas was in the Savior's presence for more than three years and never understood that Christ came *"to seek and to save the lost"* (Luke 19:10). When we sin and need forgiveness, let's not allow pride or despair to keep us from turning to God's abundant mercy (Ephesians 1:7-8).

Peter's Denial

As Jesus is taken away, Peter follows behind to join the group in the high priest's courtyard. A servant girl notices him and says he is one of Jesus' followers. Peter denies it. Another observer says the same thing; Peter denies Jesus again. A third person insists that Peter has been with Jesus. Peter denies it a third time—and a rooster crows. As Jesus turns to look at him, Peter remembers His prophetic words and walks away in tears. John's Gospel reports that another disciple, perhaps John himself, went to the courtyard with Peter. This other disciple was known to the high priest and gained access for them both (John 18:15-16). Perhaps Peter stood out to people in the crowd due to his personality, actions, or appearance. We often hear of Peter's weaknesses—his impulsiveness or boasting. Although he had been overconfident in his ability to stand firm, he did have the courage to follow Jesus to the high priest's house. The Lord always uses people who stretch their faith and go out on a limb—even if they fail. If we ask, God will always provide forgiveness and restoration.

The First Trial

Jesus endures two trials. First, He is tried by religious leaders who seek to condemn Him according to Jewish law. Jesus also faced a Roman trial in which the religious leaders accuse Him of breaking Roman law.

With such an accusation, they hope to encourage Roman citizens to favor His crucifixion. His first trial is composed of three key examinations: Jesus appears before Annas, then Caiaphas (who is joined by some members of the Sanhedrin) and finally before a formal gathering of the entire Sanhedrin (Jewish high court).

"The high priesthood of Annas and Caiaphas" (Luke 3:2) was in effect at the time of Jesus' first trial. Rome removed Annas as high priest in AD 15, though he still had great influence. His son-in-law Caiaphas stood as high priest at the time of Jesus' trial. According to Jewish law, no court could legitimately prosecute anyone in the middle of the night. Therefore, Jesus' trials before Annas and Caiaphas were actually illegal.

Jesus' enemies will do anything to get rid of Him. But, they don't want to upset the crowds who are in Jerusalem for Passover, so they hold illegal trials with Annas and Caiaphas at night. Afterward, Jesus is held at the high priest's home. Guards beat and insult Him. The religious leaders then hold a legitimate meeting of the Jewish court. They make their aim clear—they want Jesus executed. At sunrise, Jesus is brought before the Sanhedrin. Among this group of 70 men are Jewish elders, teachers of the Law, Pharisees, and Sadducees. The high priest usually leads the Sanhedrin as they sit in a semi-circle, with rabbinical students also in attendance. After a night of personal betrayal, the scattering of His disciples, confrontations with Annas and Caiaphas, and a beating from the guards, Jesus is now humiliated by a public interrogation.

Jesus' acknowledgment that He is the Messiah and the Son of God would give the Sanhedrin all the reason they need to put Him to death. Therefore, they demand, *"If you are the Christ, tell us"* (Luke 22:67). Jesus knows these leaders will not believe Him even if He tells the truth. Still, He answers, *"You say that I am"* (22:70). With confidence, Jesus' enemies now believe they will be able to put Him to death. Having heard what Jesus claims, surely more than two witnesses will testify against Him before Pontius Pilate (the Roman governor). They lead Jesus—a prisoner—one step closer to execution.

Personalize this lesson.

Prayer permeates this passage. In His time of greatest trial, Jesus not only prays for Himself—He prays for Peter, and He urges His disciples also to pray. How often do you engage in pre-emptive prayer for yourself and others? Is a friend or family member undergoing temptation? Pray for that person, using Jesus' prayer as a model. Do you personally face a faith-testing trial? Pray! Ask God to deliver you and keep you from falling.

The Passion of Christ
Luke 23

Memorize God's Word: Mark 10:45.

❖ **Luke 23:1-16; Matthew 27:15-26—Jesus Before Pilate and Herod**

1. Pontius Pilate is Judea's Roman governor. What charges do the Jews make against Jesus?

   _____

   _____

2. What is Pilate's verdict concerning Jesus?

   _____

   _____

3. Why does Pilate send Jesus to Herod?

   _____

   _____

4. Why does Herod's curiosity regarding Jesus turn to scorn?

   _____

   _____

5. How is the disagreement between Pilate and Herod resolved?

   _____

   _____

6. People today sometimes require a sign or a miracle to believe. Can you give an illustration?

_____

_____

❖ Luke 23:17-31—Barabbas Is Released; Jesus Is Condemned

7. a. Barabbas is a murderer, a rebel, and a convicted criminal. How does Pilate try to ease the mob's demands?

_____

_____

b. Why does Pilate finally yield to the people? (See also Matthew 27:15-26; John 19:12-16.)

_____

_____

8. What is the attitude of the women who follow Jesus?

_____

_____

9. How does Jesus use this episode to teach about Jerusalem's future judgment? (See also Luke 21:23-24.)

_____

_____

❖ Luke 23:32-43—The Two Thieves React to Jesus

10. How would you describe the setting of Jesus' crucifixion?

_____

_____

11. How would you describe His prayer of forgiveness?

_____

_____

12. In what way is the prophecy in Psalm 22:18 fulfilled?

_____

_____

13. What is the first criminal's attitude about Jesus?

_____

_____

14. The repentant criminal reveals his trust in Jesus. What does he gain as a result?

_____

_____

_____

❖ Luke 23:44-49—The Crucifixion

15. The first hour of the Roman day is 6:00 a.m. This passage begins at noon. What unusual physical events occur?

_____

_____

16. According to verse 46, what is Jesus' attitude?

_____

_____

17. A centurion, the women who have followed Jesus from Galilee, and several onlookers witness these events. (See also Matthew 27:56; Mark 15:40-41; John 19:25.) How do they react to what they have seen?

_____

_____

_____

❖ Luke 23:50-56; John 19:38-42—The Burial of Jesus

18. How would you describe Joseph of Arimathea?

_____

_____

19. a. Who comes with Joseph?

_____

_____

b. How do you explain why Nicodemus has been mentioned only twice previously (in chapters 3 and 7 of John), and why he comes forward now?

_____

_____

c. What do the women do?

_____

_____

Apply what you have learned. By submitting to death, Jesus, who is the Resurrection and the Life (John 11:25), knew that He would eventually conquer it. He sets the example for us who daily are called to die to ourselves, and take up our crosses and follow Him. What is God calling you to die to? What hope and help does the promise of resurrection offer to you?

The Passion of Christ
Luke 23

Jesus on Trial

In Jesus' day, the Jewish high court—the Sanhedrin—had no power to sentence a person to death. Only the Romans, who occupied Israel, could do that. Thus, after the two high priests interrogate Jesus, the religious leaders take Him to the Roman governor, Pontius Pilate, to stand trial. In front of Pilate, their accusations against Jesus are political. Earlier, the Sanhedrin had asked Him theological questions.

After questioning Him, Pilate finds *"no guilt in* [Jesus]*"* (23:4). However, the crowd continues to accuse Jesus, and Pilate doesn't know what to do. When Pilate learns Jesus is Galilean, he sees an opportunity to get out of this dilemma by sending Jesus to Herod Antipas, the Galilean ruler responsible for John the Baptist's death (Matthew 14:1-12). Because Herod's only intention is to exploit and humiliate Jesus, He does not answer any of Herod's questions.

The Sentencing

After suffering under Herod's soldiers, Jesus is returned to Pilate, who again must decide what to do about Him. Trying to satisfy the mob, Pilate, who thinks Jesus is innocent (Matthew 27:19), suggests scourging Jesus, but the mob refuses, resorting to blackmail: *"If you release this man, you are not Caesar's friend"* (John 19:12). *"Then what shall I do with Jesus?"* Pilate asks (Matthew 27:22). They yell, *"Crucify, crucify Him!"* (Luke 23:21). Pilate relents and surrenders Jesus to the mob.

Think about God's sovereignty. With Jesus' arrest, trial, and sentencing, it seemed that evil forces had won. But God used evil men's schemes to accomplish His purpose—salvation through Jesus' death on the cross. God is sovereign over your life as well. Regardless of the circumstances, He promises to work all things *"for good, for those who are called according to His purpose"* (Romans 8:28).

The Road to Calvary and the Crucifixion

In the governor's official residence, Roman soldiers strip, mock, and torture Jesus (Matthew 27:27-31), then they force Him to carry His cross through Jerusalem's streets. Carrying one's cross was done to humiliate the condemned one and to discourage onlookers from rebelling against Roman law. Because Jesus is exhausted, weak, and bleeding from His beatings, the soldiers force Simon of Cyrene to carry His cross. Along the way, despite His agony, Jesus speaks to weeping women about Jerusalem's future suffering. He is then crucified between two criminals (Isaiah 53:12) on *Golgotha* (Aramaic, *the skull*). In crucifixion, the person is laid on a cross flat on the ground; soldiers nail both his wrists to the cross, tie his feet with ropes, then drop the cross into a hole in the ground. Crucifixion is one of the cruelest forms of execution, and Jesus endured its agony for our sake. During His crucifixion, several things happen:

❖ Jesus prays for God to have mercy on all who participated in His death.

❖ Both criminals crucified beside Jesus can hear the crowd jeering Him and can see Him dying on the cross. One of them mocks the Lord along with the crowd. The other man turns to Jesus in faith and hears His assurance that *"Today you will be with Me in Paradise"* (Luke 23:43).

❖ At noon—when the sun should be its brightest—the land becomes dark for three hours.

❖ At the moment Jesus gives up His spirit, the curtain (veil) separating the Most Holy Place from the rest of the temple tears in two, from top to bottom (Matthew 27:50-51). Once a year, Israel's high priest entered the Most Holy Place in the temple where the ark of the covenant was kept. He sprinkled a sacrificed animal's blood on the cover (mercy seat) of the ark to atone for peoples' sins. According to tradition, the curtain covering this sacred place was four inches thick; two teams of oxen hitched to each side would be unable to tear it apart. Symbolically, the tearing of the curtain means that God's presence is no longer hidden. Because of Jesus' death on the cross, God's presence is now accessible to all who believe (Hebrews 10:19-22).

❖ Just before dying, Jesus calls out, *"Father, into Your hands I commit My spirit!"* (Luke 23:46). Reactions differ among the witnesses: a Roman centurion and his fellow guards declare, *"Truly this was the Son of God!"* (Matthew 27:54); the crowd leaves in anguish; and those who knew Jesus well watch from a distance.

The Burial

The body of an executed criminal was usually brought to the Valley of Gehenna and burned. Joseph of Arimathea, a member of the Sanhedrin and a secret disciple of Jesus, courageously requests Jesus' body for burial. Nicodemus, a Pharisee who secretly met with the Lord earlier, accompanies Joseph (John 19:38-39). Pilate grants Joseph's request. Because it is the day of Preparation preceding the Sabbath, and the Mosaic Law prohibited the Hebrew people from work on the Sabbath, Joseph and Nicodemus must hurry to retrieve and prepare Jesus' body. They wrap His body in linen and place it in Joseph's tomb, near the crucifixion site.

Some people struggle to understand why it was necessary for Jesus to die in order for sin to be forgiven, and mistakenly think God could simply excuse sin. But holiness and sin are as incompatible as sunlight and darkness. The Bible says, *"The wages of sin is death"* (Romans 6:23), and someone must pay those wages. Only a perfectly righteous person can die for another's sin—and that is exactly why it was necessary for Jesus to do so. The offering of Jesus' life was acceptable to God because He was the perfectly righteous One who had no sin of His own. Jesus loved us so much that He willingly suffered and died in our place. No one took His life from Him; He voluntarily gave it up for us.

Personalize this lesson.

☑ Most of the witnesses at the foot of the Cross probably thought Jesus was just like the other two men crucified with Him. But what was happening spiritually as Jesus suffered could not be seen with physical eyes. Only after the Crucifixion would people understand that God's plan for salvation had been fulfilled.

In order for sinners to come near to a holy God, sin must be forgiven, and *"without the shedding of blood there is no forgiveness"* (Hebrews 9:22). Jesus lived a perfectly obedient life; thus, He completely satisfied the need for payment for sin through His shed blood. The punishment Jesus experienced has *"brought us peace"* (Isaiah 53:5) in our relationship with God.

As you consider all Jesus has done for you at the Cross, what especially moves you? Take some time to thank Jesus and worship Him for His incredible gift of love to you. Tell Him what He means to you.

The Resurrection of Christ
Luke 24

❖ **Luke 23:55–24:1-12—The Resurrection**

1. Who goes to the tomb early on Sunday morning?

    _____

    _____

2. What is the purpose of the supplies they take with them? (See also Mark 16:1.)

    _____

    _____

3. What do they discover about the entrance and the contents of the tomb?

    _____

    _____

4. The women see *"two men stood by them in dazzling apparel"* (Luke 24:4).

    a. What is their reaction to these men?

    _____

    _____

    b. What do the men say to them?

    _____

    _____

5.   How do the women respond to this news?

_____

_____

6.   How do Jesus' disciples react when the women share this news?

_____

_____

7.   How are Peter and John's reactions alike or similar? (See also John 20:3-9.)

_____

_____

❖ Luke 24:13-24—The Road to Emmaus

8.   Jesus appears to two members of the wider group of disciples.

a.   What does this appearance tell us about God?

_____

_____

b.   How would you describe their state of mind, perception of Jesus, and what they had hoped?

_____

_____

❖ Luke 24:25-35—The Revelation Along the Road

9.   How does Jesus gently rebuke the two disciples on the road to Emmaus?

_____

_____

10. Why does Jesus remind the two disciples that *"the Christ should suffer these things and enter into His glory"* (Luke 24:26)?

_____

_____

11. What resources does Jesus use to teach these men about Himself?

_____

_____

_____

12. Jesus also appears to Simon Peter (24:34). How does this appearance encourage you?

_____

_____

_____

❖ Luke 24:36-43—Jesus Appears to All the Disciples

13. Why are the disciples so frightened at Jesus' appearance?

_____

_____

14. How do Jesus' initial questions reassure the disciples?

_____

_____

15. What are the similarities and differences between Jesus' resurrection body and His earthly body?

_____

_____

_____

16. Based on this passage and 1 John 3:2, what will our resurrected bodies be like?

_____

_____

_____

❖ Luke 24:44-53—Jesus Explains the Scriptures

17. How does Jesus help the disciples understand the teachings about Him recorded in the Law of Moses, the Prophets, and the Psalms?

_____

_____

18. What message and mission does Jesus give His followers?

_____

_____

19. What command and promise does Jesus give His disciples concerning their mission? (See also Acts 1:4, 8.)

_____

_____

20. How would you describe Jesus' departure as recorded in these verses and in Acts 1:9-11?

_____

_____

21. What two evidences of faith and obedience to Christ do the disciples show?

_____

_____

Apply what you have learned. Unless God helps us, we often miss the wonderful things that are right in front of us. The men on the road to Emmaus didn't recognize Jesus until *"their eyes were opened"* (verse 31). And the disciples didn't understand all that Jesus had taught them about Himself until *"He opened their minds to understand the Scriptures"* (verse 45). Do you assume you "get it" with no extra help? Why not ask God to open your eyes and heart to the wonderful things you may be missing?

The Resurrection of Christ
Luke 24

Earlier, we read of the faithful, courageous women who watched Jesus' crucifixion (Luke 23:49). After Joseph of Arimathea took the Lord's body down from the cross, the women followed him to the tomb where Jesus was laid, then prepared spices for His burial. Now, in this exciting final chapter, Luke describes the disciples' reaction to the news of their Master's resurrection.

He Has Risen

The women at the tomb that life-changing Sunday morning include Mary Magdalene, Joanna, wife of Herod's steward, and Mary, James's mother. Some tombs were caves sealed by huge stones (Matthew 27:59-60). Bodies were usually wrapped in long linen strips covered with spices (John 19:40). People often honored their dead by going to their tombs after the Sabbath to apply more spices, just as these women intend to do. But the stone no longer covers the tomb's entrance, and the women are shocked to find their Master's body gone! Seeing two men John describes as *"angels"* (John 20:12), they bow low in fear. The men ask, *"Why do you seek the living among the dead? He is not here, but has risen"* (Luke 24:5).

Each Gospel contains different details of Jesus' resurrection. John says that when Peter and John hear the news, they run to the tomb. John sees the linen strips lying there; Peter also notes the folded burial cloth that had covered Jesus' head (John 20:1-9). Matthew reports an earthquake that occurs when an angel rolls back the stone, terrifying the Roman guards. The guards report these facts to the chief priests, who bribe them to spread the lie that Jesus' disciples stole His body (Matthew 28:4, 11-15). In Mark's Gospel we see the angel instructing the women to tell the disciples Jesus is going ahead of them to Galilee (Mark 16:7). Mary Magdalene's encounter with Jesus and His second appearance to the disciples are told in John 20:10-18, 24-28. Luke alone tells of the two disciples on the road to Emmaus who meet with Jesus. The various Gospel accounts can be compared to viewing different broadcasts of a single event today. Each camera films the same scene from its unique perspective.

The Road to Emmaus

That same day, two of Jesus' followers are walking from Jerusalem to Emmaus, a village seven miles away. Like the other disciples, they are sad and confused. Jesus joins them, but they don't recognize Him. After they tell this "stranger" what has occurred, Jesus gently reproves them, explaining all that the Scriptures say of Him. Nearing Emmaus, they urge Him to stay with them. Note that Jesus waits to be invited—He is gracious and never forces Himself on anyone. Only as they sit at the table and Jesus blesses and breaks the bread do the two recognize Him. As soon as He disappears, they hurry back to Jerusalem to share this good news with the other disciples.

Think about how often we have been like the two disciples on the road to Emmaus—distraught over some devastating circumstance in our lives. When we recognize Jesus' presence as we walk with Him, and remember what He has done for us, we will praise Him. These men recognize Him and become among the first in a long line of Christian witnesses. The dangers of a night journey don't stop them from sharing their good news. Are you eager to share what you know about Jesus? Don't be afraid to go out and tell others who are still "in the dark."

Reunion and Reminder

During this time, Jesus also appears to Simon Peter, knowing Peter needs to be reassured of His love and forgiveness. As the two men from Emmaus tell the Eleven the good news, Jesus suddenly stands among them and says, *"Peace to you"* (24:36). The scared disciples think He is a ghost, and Jesus asks them why they doubt. Some there still don't believe the glad reports of the women, these two men, and Simon Peter. The Lord invites them to look at His hands and feet and even touch Him, so they can know He truly is their risen Lord and Master.

In His glorified body, Jesus can eat, appear and disappear, and pass through closed doors. We do not know if our resurrected bodies will be as similar to our present bodies as was Christ's. The fact is, His body needed to be recognizable to those still on earth. Paul's teaching on resurrected bodies implies that they will be as different from mortal bodies as plants are from their seeds. *"So is it with the resurrection of the dead. What is sown is perishable; what is raised is imperishable. It is sown in dishonor; it is raised in glory. It is sown in weakness; it is raised in power. It is sown a natural body; it is raised a spiritual body. If there is a natural body, there is also a spiritual body"* (1 Corinthians 15:42-44).

Luke concludes with a brief account of the events between the Resurrection and the Ascension. One might think they all happen on the day of Jesus' resurrection. But in the first chapter Acts Luke explains that Christ taught the disciples for more than 40 days after His resurrection. He helped them understand that everything that had befallen Him was a fulfillment of Scripture, including the Law of Moses, the Prophets, and the Psalms.

The Ascension

Christ's ascension 40 days after His resurrection is yet another demonstration of God's power. The Holy Spirit's presence and power is available today to all believers (John 16:7). All who receive Christ receive the same Holy Spirit (Romans 8:9-11). After Christ ascends into heaven, the disciples return to Jerusalem with joy, praising God. Are we who know the Lord and have the gift of the Holy Spirit so filled with Him that our joy is full (John 15:11), and we continually praise Him (Psalm 103)?

Personalize this lesson.

It is fitting that this wonderful gospel of Jesus ends with a blessing. Jesus lifts up His hands to bless His disciples and, in a final act of blessing, He is carried up to heaven. The disciples' response? They return *"to Jerusalem with great joy and were continually ... blessing God"* (verse 53). Think of all the ways God has blessed you through your study of Luke. Write them down. Take your time and let these blessings soak in and stir up your joy. Then respond by blessing God in return. Imagine His joy!

Small Group Leader's Guide

While *Engaging God's Word* is great for personal study, it is generally even more effective and enjoyable when studied with others. Studying with others provides different perspectives and insights, care, prayer support, and fellowship that studying on your own does not. Depending on your personal circumstances, consider studying with your family or spouse, with a friend, in a Sunday school, with a small group at church, work, or in your neighborhood, or in a mentoring relationship.

In a traditional Community Bible Study class, your study would involve a proven four-step method: personal study, a small group discussion facilitated by a trained leader, a lecture covering the passage of Scripture, and a written commentary about the same passage. *Engaging God's Word* provides two of these four steps with the study questions and commentary. When you study with a group, you add another of these—the group discussion. And if you enjoy teaching, you could even provide a modified form of the fourth, the lecture, which in a small group setting might be better termed a wrap-up talk.

Here are some suggestions to help leaders facilitate a successful group study.

1. Decide how long you would like each group meeting to last. For a very basic study, without teaching, time for fellowship, or group prayer, plan on one hour. If you want to allow for fellowship before the meeting starts, add at least 15 minutes. If you plan to give a short teaching, add 15 or 20 minutes. If you also want time for group prayer, add another 10 or 15 minutes. Depending on the components you include for your group, each session will generally last between one and two hours.

2. Set a regular time and place to meet. Meeting in a church classroom or a conference room at work is fine. Meeting in a home is also a good option, and sometimes more relaxed and comfortable.

3. Publicize the study and/or personally invite people to join you.

4. Begin praying for those who have committed to come. Continue to pray for them individually throughout the course of the study.

5. Make sure everyone has his or her own book at least a week before you meet for the first time.

6. Encourage group members to read the first lesson and do the questions before they come to the group meeting.

7. Prepare your own lesson.

8. Prepare your wrap-up talk, if you plan to give one. Here is a simple process for developing a wrap-up talk:

   a. Divide the passage you are studying into two or three divisions. Jot down the verses for each division and describe the content of each with one complete sentence that answers the question, "What is the passage about?"

   b. Decide on the central idea of your wrap-up talk. The central idea is the life-changing principle found in the passage that you believe God wants to implant in the hearts and minds of your group. The central idea answers the question, "What does God want us to learn from this passage?"

   c. Provide one illustration that would make your central idea clear and meaningful to your group. This could be an illustration from your own life, or a story you've read or heard somewhere else.

   d. Suggest one application that would help your group put the central idea into practice.

   e. Choose an aim for your wrap-up talk. The aim answers the question, "What does God want us to do about it?" It encourages specific change in your group's lives, if they choose to respond to the central idea of the passage. Often it takes the form of a question you will ask your group: "Will you, will I choose to … ?"

9. Show up early to the study so you can arrange the room, set up the refreshments (if you are serving any), and welcome people as they arrive.

10. Whether your meeting includes a fellowship time or not, begin the discussion time promptly each week. People appreciate it when you respect their time. Transition into the discussion with prayer, inviting God to guide the discussion time and minister personally to each person present.

11. Model enthusiasm to the group. Let them know how excited you are about what you are learning—and your eagerness to hear what God is teaching them.

12. As you lead through the questions, encourage everyone to participate, but don't force anyone. If one or two people tend to dominate the discussion, encourage quieter ones to participate by saying something like, "Let's hear from someone who hasn't shared yet." Resist the urge to teach during discussion time. This time is for your group to share what they have been discovering.

13. Try to allow time after the questions have been discussed to talk about the "Apply what you have learned," "Think about" and "Personalize this lesson" sections. Encourage your group members in their efforts to partner with God in allowing Him to transform their lives.

14. Transition into the wrap-up talk, if you are doing one (see number 8).

15. Close in prayer. If you have structured your group to allow time for prayer, invite group members to pray for themselves and one another, especially focusing on the areas of growth they would like to see in their lives as a result of their study. If you have not allowed time for group prayer, you as leader can close this time.

16. Before your group finishes their final lesson, start praying and planning for what your next *Engaging God's Word* study will be.

About Community Bible Study

For almost 40 years Community Bible Study has taught the Word of God through in-depth, community-based Bible studies. With nearly 700 classes in the United States as well as classes in more than 70 countries, Community Bible Study purposes to be an "every-person's Bible study, available to all."

Classes for men, women, youth, children, and even babies, are all designed to make members feel loved, cared for, and accepted—regardless of age, ethnicity, socio-economic status, education, or church membership. Because Bible study is most effective in one's heart language, Community Bible Study curriculum has been translated into more than 50 languages.

Community Bible Study makes every effort to stand in the center of the mainstream of historic Christianity, concentrating on the essentials of the Christian faith rather than denominational distinctives. Community Bible Study respects different theological views, preferring to focus on helping people to know God through His Word, grow deeper in their relationships with Jesus, and be transformed into His likeness.

Community Bible Study's focus ... is to glorify God by providing in-depth Bible studies and curriculum in a Christ-centered, grace-filled, and philosophically safe environment.

Community Bible Study's passion ... is the transformation of individuals, families, communities, and generations through the power of God's Word, making disciples of the Lord Jesus Christ.

Community Bible Study's relationship with local churches ... is one of support and respect. Community Bible Study classes are composed of people from many different churches; they are designed to complement and not compete with the ministry of the local church. Recognizing that the Lord has chosen the local church as His primary channel of ministry, Community Bible Study encourages class members to belong to and actively support their local churches and to be servants and leaders in their congregations.

Do you want to experience lasting transformation in your life? Are you ready to go deeper in God's Word? There is probably a Community Bible Study near you! Find out by visiting www.findmyclass.org or scan the QR code on this page.

For more information:

Call   800-826-4181

Email info@communitybiblestudy.org

Web   www.communitybiblestudy.org

Class www.findmyclass.org

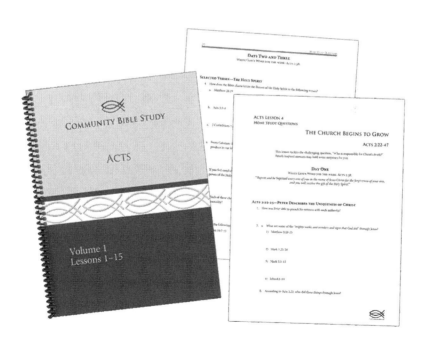

Where will your next Bible study adventure take you?

Engage Bible Studies help you discover the joy
and the richness of God's Word and apply it your life.

Check out these titles for your next adventure:

Engaging God's Word: Genesis

Engaging God's Word: Deuteronomy

Engaging God's Word: Joshua & Judges

Engaging God's Word: Daniel

Engaging God's Word: Job

Engaging God's Word: Mark

Engaging God's Word: Luke

Engaging God's Word: Acts

Engaging God's Word: Romans

Engaging God's Word: Galatians

Engaging God's Word: Ephesians

Engaging God's Word: Philippians

Engaging God's Word: Colossians

Engaging God's Word: 1 & 2 Thessalonians

Engaging God's Word: Hebrews

Engaging God's Word: James

Engaging God's Word: 1 & 2 Peter

Engaging God's Word: Revelation

Available at Amazon.com and in fine bookstores.

Visit engagebiblestudies.com

Made in the USA
Columbia, SC
03 September 2023

22442642R00139